the
Shopping
Diet

G

GALLERY BOOKS

New York

London

Toronto

Sydney

the Shopping Diet

Spend Less and Get More

Phillip Bloch

Gallery Books
A Division of Simon & Schuster, Inc.
1230 Avenue of the Americas
New York, NY 10020

Copyright © 2010 by Phillip Bloch

First Gallery Books trade paperback edition August 2010

GALLERY BOOKS and colophon are trademarks of Simon & Schuster, Inc.

For information about special discounts for bulk purchases, please contact Simon & Schuster Special Sales at 1-866-506-1949 or business@ simonandschuster.com.

The Simon & Schuster Speakers Bureau can bring authors to your live event. For more information or to book an event, contact the Simon & Schuster Speakers Bureau at 1-866-248-3049 or visit our website at www.simonspeakers.com.

Designed by Jaime Putorti
Illustrations by Jason Snyder
Shopping bags image courtesy of istockphoto.com

Manufactured in the United States of America

10   9   8   7   6   5   4   3   2   1

Library of Congress Cataloging-in-Publication Data

Bloch, Phillip.
    The shopping diet : spend less and get more / By Phillip Bloch.
        p. cm.
    1. Shopping 2. Clothing and dress 3. Clothes closets. I. Title
    TT507.B577 2010
    746.9'2—dc22

                                                        2010012648

ISBN 978-1-4391-1026-3
ISBN 978-1-4391-5054-2 (ebook)

To all the people in every shape, size, and color that I've known and loved, whether you have been family, friends, clients, or fans, who have contributed, shared, and enhanced my life, career, and my gift of style. You have each in your own way enriched me and truly made this book possible. Individually and collectively, your generosity, words of wisdom, praise, and criticism are gifts that mean the world to me.

Contents

Foreword

by Simon Doonan

Creative Director of Barneys New York
and author of *Eccentric Glamour*

It happened in the early 1960s. I was ten years old and I fell in love for the first time.

My uncle Dave had a girlfriend. Her name was Irma. She wore leopard slacks with lots of jangly jewelry and she had a giant teased beehive. She looked a bit like a blond Amy Winehouse. My sister and I worshipped her. We did not care that her hair was fake or that it looked like a bird's nest on steroids. Watching Irma take off her beehive every night and stick it on the mantelpiece next to her gin bottle and her unpaid bills was the highlight of our glamour-starved lives.

There it would sit until the next morning when the great reattachment ceremony would take place. Once it was pinned and sprayed, Irma would light a cigarette and strut off to her job, her incredibly gorgeous orgasmic job.

Irma worked in a dress shop. The name was, if I recall correctly, *Modes de Paree*. This is where it happened. This is where I fell in love . . . with fashion.

There were probably dead flies in the window of *Modes de Paree* and broken fingers on the mannequins, but to my ten-year-old eyes, this was the most glamorous place in the universe. Watching Irma transform her customers and send them back out into the world, empowered, more confident, and more alive, was a mystical experience. I was hooked. I was mesmerized. The goddess of shopping had revealed herself to me. I was an instant convert.

Shopping for fashion is a totally magical process. It's a ritual of reinvention and rebirth. Old skins are shed. Optimism is rekindled. Dreams are fulfilled. Sheesh! No wonder it's so insanely addictive!

In the last few years, shopping has become central to our culture in a way that would have blown Irma's beehive right off her head if she were alive to see it. Red carpet obsessions and designer names dominate the media, fueling our now out-of-control addiction to clothing and accessories. Many women feel overwhelmed, exhausted, burned out, and spent out.

Enter Phillip Bloch.

Phillip is an unusual bloke. He combines a passion for fashion with a wildly pragmatic sensibility. Phillip understands the transformative magic of shopping. He revels in it. He celebrates fashion as a form of creative expression, but he also brings order, sanity, and a much needed dollop of rational thinking to the whole process.

It's a shame that Phillip never had the chance to meet Irma. She could really have used his help. Though he would probably have given her beehive a thumbs-up, I think he would have hated her approach to customer service. Irma was a ferocious saleswoman who only cared about flogging the merch. Some of her customers came off better than others. Irma prided herself on her ability to foist stuff onto people regardless of how horrible it looked. "It's a perfect fit, madam," she would say, secretly grabbing handfuls of loose fabric at the small of her customer's back.

Unlike my commission-crazed auntie, Phillip really cares that you look your best. His mission is a simple one: Let the women of America fall in love with fashion and fulfill their style potential!

Introduction

You promised yourself you wouldn't give into temptation. You swore up and down to all your friends, "I've got it under control."

But here it is, staring you right in the face—that over-priced monster-size handbag that you can't afford, yet you couldn't walk away from it, either. *And* the designer black skirt that may or may not happen to look exactly like the ten others in your closet, even if you insist it's the most slimming black skirt known to womankind. Oh, and what about those new jeans? I know, I know: Not only are they as life sustaining as food and air, but they were also on sale.

You've done this over and over again. Binge shopping. And now you are bloated and drunk with remorse, realizing that your consumerism is out of control. Something has to give. Whether you realize it or not, it's time to shake hands with some cold facts. You can't afford another freewheeling shopping spree. Now is the time to take a deeper look into the mirror. Do you like what you see?

Look, the joy of shopping is no mystery to me. I was born to shop. I'm genetically predisposed. Even in elementary school, I magically and mysteriously knew how to navigate my way through the sales racks and the ready-to-wear collections. However, nothing would be purchased and make it back to Chez Bloch unless it was not only gorgeous but also useful and, in my eyes, transformational. The concept of versatility—taking an ensemble from boardroom to ballroom—has always been important to me. I have always had the uncanny ability of knowing what works for different people's body types and lifestyles.

Transforming my passion for fashion into a career, I have been lucky enough to know clothing and style from many different points of view, including as a model, author, style commentator, and designer. As Hollywood's premiere fashion stylist, I have dressed some of the world's biggest stars for some of the most important moments in their lives. When I've gotten celebrities, such as Halle Berry, Jim Carrey, Drew Barrymore, Jennifer Lopez, John Travolta, and Nicole Kidman, ready for a big event, I have always had unlimited resources—think trunk loads of top designers. Still, I'm never wasteful. The same is true for all my design projects. Whether it's the jewelry line I sold on QVC or the men's shoes I created for Hush Puppies, I always aim to provide real people with multiple amazing-looking options that won't blow their budgets. In the tips I'm asked to give for fashion magazines like *InStyle, Elle,* and *Vogue,* I consistently preach versatility and affordable fashion. I'm able to do this because over my years of working in Hollywood, I have amassed the best insider secrets when it comes to shopping and dressing women and men.

Listen, when you overeat, your doctor or your friends suggest that you go on a diet. But what happens when you overspend? Who is there to rein you in and give the advice you need? Well, with the help of this book, you now have me! And I'm going to put you on a diet—*The Shopping Diet*! It's a ten-step plan that will help you spend less and get more by looking at your shopping and spending habits from a whole new angle. My well-thought-out, approachable, and easy tips will take you to the next style level and shrink those credit card bills. You can retain your individual style, and even improve it, without breaking the bank. It's not your waistline we'll whittle, but your bottom line.

In this volatile economic climate, we all have to reevaluate our power to purchase. Like any successful weight-loss plan, *The Shopping Diet* is a lifestyle change and not a quick-fix fad diet. It begins by analyzing the hidden reasons for your shopping problem. Then *The Diet* tackles the symptoms: overflowing, disorganized, and cluttered closets. After effectively cleaning your closets, you can move on to restocking your wardrobe without falling back into old, bad habits of overspending. When shopping is not a compulsion, but rather a nourishing experience or occasional treat, it feels better, tastes sweeter, and looks fantastic.

The Shopping Diet offers a lifetime of shopping success by:

* Unveiling your shopping compulsions
* Reevaluating and accentuating the positive in your personal style and body type
* Making your current wardrobe work for you
* Teaching you how to maximize your purchases
* Offering the gift of conscious spending

Now, on to the first step!

part one

Digest This:

Weigh the Past for a Beautiful Future

Step One:

Admit You're an Overshopper

It's hard to resist buying compulsively when the world is one big Willy Wonka Chocolate Factory of clothes, shoes, and sparkling accessories. Now more than ever, it's *not* okay to carelessly throw a random pair of sunglasses or another bottle of perfume into your cart just because they're there and they sparkle and you love them . . . or you at least love the packaging.

We all have access to shopping twenty-four hours a day, seven days a week. For anyone with a penchant for overshopping, temptation is constantly calling in the form of shiny window displays, the barrage of store catalogs in your mailbox, and online offers clogging your email inbox. Credit cards are the fuel for this raging fire. It has become abundantly clear in the last few years that credit card companies want nothing more than to give us a gazillion dollars in credit, wait until we miss a minimum payment or don't read the fine print in the contracts, and then let interest rates soar. Living on credit can be an oh-too-alluring trap, especially with the credit card companies' appealing incentives of travel miles and luxurious rewards. Time and time again, you have heard that all that glitters is not gold (or even platinum, despite what your credit card would infer). But if you keep overcharging on your AmEx, you might end up buried in the red. The result: If you don't pay off your bill for that $10 tank top when the first invoice arrives, it can end up costing you $100 within the year, thanks to fluctuating and unpredictable interest rates.

Even worse than paying ten times more than what you thought you spent on a flimsy top, unfettered credit can lead to no credit at all. If you can't keep up with your spending, your assets could quickly become your liabilities. Your credit card could be canceled, plummeting your fragile credit score. Down the road, when you really need a line of credit to purchase something imperative (a new apartment, a new car, etc.), you'll find yourself in a real jam. Do you realize that some companies even look at your credit score when you apply for a job?

If you face credit problems, you are not alone. The average person's debt in the United States has risen to a staggering number. Recently, banks have been starting to dig even deeper than your credit score in order to determine eligibility for loans or more credit. In fact, overall accumulated debt is starting to be assessed and considered an equally important deciding factor. But you can beat the statistics by facing your shopping problem. If you are feeling powerless over your shopping habits and overspending, trust me, you can move beyond it. I'm here to see to it that you don't waste another dollar on things you don't need. Once you realize that your goal in life is not to buy the *most* things but to buy the best, the rest will become easier.

The first step in conquering any problem is to admit that

you have one. However positive or negative the current economy may be, it is crucial to learn from the way you use, and possibly abuse, your finances when it comes to shopping. Do you have a problem? And if so, how bad is it? Treat your experiences of past irresponsible shopping as you would a new pair of shoes—you already paid for them mentally and financially, so you might as well put them to use.

Food for Thought

The Shopping Diet will only work for you if you make it work. So throughout the book, I will ask you to reflect honestly on your own habits. This will lead to a self-awareness where you will then be able to use the solutions provided in each step. Here are a few questions about how you shop:

* Do you shop with a list or do you buy on the fly?
* When purchasing an item, do you bother to take into account whether you already own something similar?
* When budgeting for shopping, are you relying on the Psychic Network or tapping into your own ESP (Extra Spending Powers) to predict how to spend future income that may never even materialize?

Shopping Reality Check

Whether your buying sprees would make a celebutante heiress blush or you feel you simply shop unwisely, there's a lot to be learned by analyzing your spending patterns. This will take a little detective work. First, collect your bank statements, credit card bills, and receipts from the past six months. If you don't keep those types of documents, you should! Start collecting them immediately and do the following exercise after one month (then repeat after three months).

I want you to answer these questions about your spending habits as honestly as you can. They are here to help you understand where and when you shop till you drop. No one else has to see them. Habits become clearer once you really look at the cold hard facts.

Find and write down your three most budget-busting shopping sprees. Whether it was only an hour or a two-day frenzy, record the date, how long the spree lasted, and the total amount that you spent.

1. _____

2. _____

3. _____

Reflect on each one of these sprees by identifying the items that you bought. Were these items planned or unplanned purchases? And were they necessary or unnecessary?

1. _____

2. _____

3. _____

Now that you've listed the items you purchased and addressed whether they were needed, continue on your reality check and see if these items were appropriate purchases or excessive. For example, you may have needed new water glasses, but did you really have to buy a service of twenty? Or did they really need to have the same designer label as your shirt? Did you end up loving your purchases as much as you thought you would in the store (the answer might be yes, and that's okay)? We're working on perspective, so we need to dig even deeper than your receipt pile.

What's Eating You? ⌒

Like an overeater who uses food as an emotional outlet, you need to figure out what compels you to whip out that credit card. You need to understand the way you shop. You need to know *why* you buy, buy, and buy again so that the next time you actually have the power and knowledge to resist. Those shoes look sexy when they're on the shelf and on sale. You think you can afford them, so you quickly buy them. But the euphoric endorphin rush passes when you put them in your closet and realize once again that you have way too many shoes in the first place. And though they may have been on sale, were they really a bargain? That question will quickly be answered with the arrival of the credit card bill . . . and subsequently, any remaining good feelings will come to a screeching halt. You don't want to be a part of that merry-go-round anymore, so let's get off that ride by figuring out your triggers.

Many people suffer from low self-esteem issues and don't believe that they deserve to have happiness in their lives. But far too many people in this celebrity-inspired, egocentric, and attention-grabbing culture also suffer unconsciously from habits of overindulgence and gluttony. While these two traits may seem in opposition to each other, both are often a manifestation of the same syndrome of overcompensation. Both come from an unhealthy place of unnecessarily wanting to prove and validate oneself to others.

As the Dr. Phil of Fashion, I don't have to pick your brain to find out the true psychological issues of why you shop and spend too much. And I'm sure you don't want to deal with a label, either (unless it's a designer one on a piece of clothing). You are willing to go on *The Shopping Diet,* which is good enough for me. However, in my business, I hear men and women talk about everything under the sun, especially shopping. And after years of listening to clients who range from PTA moms to celebrity icons, I have boiled down the causes for overshopping to four basic motivations: childhood habits, the opposite sex, low self-esteem, and competition. Let's analyze.

CHILDHOOD HABITS

If you think about it long enough, you can usually trace the roots of your feelings about shopping back to your parents. There are far too many adults who were dragged to malls and department stores when they were children. There was no babysitter, so Macy's became their playground. I have a friend whose mother was the belle of the ball on the cocktail party circuit in her little hometown. The mister of the house was a prominent physician. Saturdays for this little girl were not spent as quality time with her parents, baking cookies with mom or four-wheeling with dad. Love and attention came in the form of mom's shopping trips for the dress with tulle that would have made Bjork's Oscar swan gown look like an understated shift, followed by hours of trying on patent leather Mary Janes in various department stores.

Some adults got the stamp of approval to "shop till you drop" from watching their parents do the same thing. Family outings were composed of carrying heavy shopping bags until the handles became engraved into their palms. These people remember their parents buying lavish items week after week and therefore associate possessions with happiness. Conversely, there is another type of child whose family could perhaps not afford the finer things in life and struggled to make ends meet. This child felt deprived of what everyone else seemed to possess, which becomes the driving force in adulthood. These people buy to prove to themselves and to others that they are valid and valuable. Both of these types of children grew up into adults who feel like shopping is their God-granted mission in life. They may pay minimums on their high-balance credit cards, yet there's no stopping them from cruising the mall for the latest goods each weekend and overcompensating by overbuying. The connection to their parents is intrinsically linked to the excitement of purchasing. As adults, they will never stop spending in their futile efforts to try to re-create or validate the past.

Do you want to return to simpler childhood times by heading into a store? The only problem is now daddy no longer foots the bill—you do. It is time to do a life update because you cannot afford to continue down memory lane.

THE OPPOSITE SEX

You only get one chance to make a first impression. The truth is that the first moment of connection with a potential significant other is purely based on image projection—as are most initial meetings. The visual attraction will hopefully stimulate a physical attraction, which will perhaps in turn transform into an emotional one. So it makes sense that most of us are obsessed with what we wear and how we present ourselves, even if perhaps some of us act like we're not (that, too, is just an act).

When getting ready for that first date, you inevitably want to display your feminine wiles, yet you don't want to look like you're getting ready for a photo shoot with *Playboy.* Yes, you want people to love you. But do you ever let the real you show up? Or do you just keep sending a false representative out of your closet to do your PR? You might be having dinner with the person of your dreams in an outfit emulating the latest fashion magazine cover or your favorite film or pop star. But we know that entire look came with a huge price.

Women love a man who dresses up for a date, but guys don't see things in quite the same way. Most men, in fact, are not requesting anyone perfect. They're just looking for a woman who they can work with and is worth it. The truth of the matter is that the guy eating that burger across the table from you is looking hard at that designer bag of yours thinking, *I know that I can afford the meal, but can I afford her?* High maintenance comes with a high price. You might end up pushing him away when he's actually a man you want to pull in closer.

So, girls, before you go gallivanting off to make your next Galliano purchase, here is a little something to consider: A man really just cares about what you look like in clothes (and even more about how you look *out* of them). It doesn't matter to him if those clothes are designer or discount. As long as they fit you and you're looking smoking hot, you will be fitting for him. If he asks you to dress to impress, it's rarely for himself. It's for when you meet his family, his friends, or his boss. Believe me, if the man had his way and had you all to himself, you probably wouldn't be wearing many clothes at all! It's time to realize he's not reading your designer labels. A real man worth his weight in gold isn't interested in who you're wearing but how you're wearing it.

LOW SELF-ESTEEM

The regular girl (size 12–14, because that is the American average) probably dreads shopping because she doesn't look like anyone she sees on TV, on film, or in magazines. It becomes an excuse to let herself go. Girls who are full figured can turn themselves into self-saboteurs. The shopping and eating become a never-ending cycle of guilt. These shoppers shop because they're unhappy about themselves. Then they eat because they're unhappy that they shopped so much. This unhappiness is only exacerbated when they can't fit into the items they bought due to their overeating. "I eat because I'm unhappy and I'm unhappy because I eat" is a vicious cycle.

Do you tell yourself that Ben, Jerry, the Keebler Elves, and Aunt Jemima aren't judging? Do you tell yourself that the designers are the ones to blame because they don't make clothes for your body type and shape? Or that the stores are at fault because they are not selling clothes for the "real" woman? The reality is that much of this attitude stems from self-loathing. These girls find temporary happiness in the things that don't have a clothing size—the expensive skin creams, the dazzling earrings, the designer pumps, the endless pairs of stockings, tummy tuckers, and booty lifters. But all the shape shifters in the world aren't going to put you in a permanently perfect mental shape. First and foremost, you need to believe in yourself—whether this renewed sense of self-esteem comes from a concerted effort to lose the economic, emotional, and physical weight or from simply becoming content with who you are. At least come to terms and be honest with your feelings. Suddenly, it won't be about what you have or don't have, but about the limitless possibilities you have opened yourself up to.

COMPETITION

I've heard women talk about shopping like it is a competitive sport. They're out with their girlfriends and one finds a great silk shirt on sale, so naturally another has to buy something even more fabulous that either costs a lot more or was an even bigger bargain. Now the race is on to find anything of value before you leave, including those olive green D'Orsay pumps that you'll never wear because you have no idea what

> ## BLOCH**BUSTER TIP**
>
>
>
> Before buying any last-minute item, ask yourself, "Do I really need this? What is its perceived value compared to what it's really worth? In what way will this item add value to my look . . . or my life?" Nine times out of ten, your answers to these three questions will make you put that little item back.

to pair them with in your wardrobe. How would life be fair if your girlfriend got the great sale item and you walked out of the store after hours of dedicated digging with nothing more than sore feet? Oh, the pain of those unproductive shopping hours!

The whole idea of competition is semi-self-defeating. If you keep looking back to see if someone is catching up, you'll miss where you're going. If a girlfriend finds something beautiful, be happy for her treasure. Maybe you'll be the one next time who hits the big prize. The bottom line is that shopping is never a competition and you can quickly waste a lot of hard-earned money trying to match your friends, purchase for purchase. And if you and your girlfriend are really good friends, I'm sure she'll let you borrow that steal of a shirt, anyway!

You have come to see that your spending actually has patterns. And I'm not talking about bold floral ones. It's time to raise your consciousness like André Courrèges raised hemlines with the miniskirt and start making informed purchases. Courrèges showed a lot more leg . . . you need to show a lot more sense! When watching your weight, you always consider the caloric intake of the things you eat and imagine how it will affect your body weight. Similarly in shopping, it's the economical and emotional weight of your purchase that you must consider so that you don't get caught in the same shopping traps again and again. I promise that when you sort through the free-for-all in your closet and change your thought process, your buying and shopping habits will change, your budget will be greener, and your stress levels will be leaner. You have taken that first step by admitting to an overabundance of clothing and stuff that is just waiting to be reassessed and reworked . . . or removed.

Look in the mirror and say the following words out loud: *My goal is to have the knowledge to shop safely and responsibly, and the ability to remain true to my budget through working the steps of* The Shopping Diet.

Okay, now let's turn that motivation into real commitment with the next big step.

Step Two:

Commit to *The Diet*

Most people would love to stop their out-of-control shopping and spending habits. But are they earnestly trying to find solutions and committing to them? Well, you are! You are going to review and sign a contract with yourself. You will be taking your goal of shopping on a budget without giving up on style from just a concept to actual action.

To do that, we have to take a trip back in shopping time. Remember the days of layaway, before we were all so caught up in surfing the web and drowning in credit card debt? Back then, if you loved a dress so much, you just dropped off $10 per week at the department store until you paid it off. You had to sign an agreement with the store, committing yourself to that dress. You knew exactly how much it cost, and you had to pay cash. There was no way to impulse buy on layaway.

Well, I want you to sign a layaway agreement with yourself. You are committing to a big change in your relationship to shopping and spending. Think about it: Layaway represents all the right things about shopping. It means you only buy the right things on a schedule that works for you. It's a serious plan with a worthwhile reward.

THE SHOPPING DIET CONTRACT

YOUR NAME:

ITEM ON LAYAWAY: One well-stocked, well-organized, well-edited wardrobe.

PAYMENT METHOD: Commitment and determination.

INITIAL DEPOSIT: Acknowledging your bad shopping habits and making an effort to change through a desire to get your finances and spending under control.

PAYMENT ONE: Clean out your mental and physical closets.

PAYMENT TWO: Become reacquainted with your wardrobe and your body type.

PAYMENT THREE: Identify your needs (no, silver heels do not count as work shoes). Learn to differentiate between what you need and what you love.

PAYMENT FOUR: Reinvent the pieces of clothing you once loved so that you can reinvigorate your wardrobe.

PAYMENT FIVE: Establish a realistic budget and go shopping for the pieces that you lack.

PAYOFF: Accept all the compliments on your wonderful wardrobe and in-control attitude while looking your best and enjoying life to its fullest.

I agree to all of the layaway terms stated above.

SIGNATURE _____ DATE _____

Clothing Journal

In the same way a new diet asks you to keep a record of everything you eat in a food journal, you're going to write down everything you wear, day and night, for two weeks. This will help you understand your outfits as well as exactly what you need to discard and buy in order to have a completely well-balanced wardrobe. It will also help in determining your overall style. I'm not one for giving out homework assignments, but look at it this way—there will be a field trip! *We will go shopping* . . . after you have a clean and organized closet. You can take your money to the bank on that one. After you record what you wear, you're going to reassess and redetermine your own style. It's time to find out what's going on with your body, from head to toe, including shoes, accessories, bras, and underwear. Use the following pages to act as a journal to catalog your outfits. Be sure to be descriptive (color, style, etc.) for maximum benefit.

Week One

SUNDAY

A.M.

P.M.

MONDAY

A.M.

P.M.

TUESDAY

A.M.

P.M.

WEDNESDAY

A.M.

P.M.

THURSDAY

A.M.

P.M.

FRIDAY

A.M.

P.M.

SATURDAY

A.M.

P.M.

Week Two

SUNDAY

A.M.

P.M.

MONDAY

A.M.

P.M.

TUESDAY

A.M.

P.M.

WEDNESDAY

A.M.

P.M.

THURSDAY

A.M.

P.M.

FRIDAY

A.M.

P.M.

SATURDAY

A.M.

P.M.

BLOCHBUSTER TIP

Recording what you wear every day is a great way to get to know what pieces you actually own and use. Next time you hit the stores, bring your journal along so that you don't overspend on items that won't get much use.

Again, I want to congratulate you. You have taken the first steps toward financial freedom and fashion fabulousness. By committing to your goal and signing a contract to that end, you (and not your charge cards) are in charge. You will reach a new level of self-confidence because you're finally taking the time to address the problem. You're on the road to retail redemption and a brand-new reality . . . a reality that you can actually afford. Your goal of getting a handle on your spending and shopping habits through the steps of *The Shopping Diet* is moving forward. In addition to your patterns of spending, you have started to figure out your dressing patterns—what you feel comfortable in, your everyday faves, the items that never get play. You know what you like to wear. Now you need to sort out what actually looks *good* on you.

Step Three:

Know Your Personal Style and Body

I'm sure you're a woman of style, but this chapter will help you determine exactly *what* style. Are you a classic or a rebel when it comes to the image you wish to project to the world? Step Three helps you to determine your look so that you're not schizophrenically shopping all over the place and buying items that don't add up to clever outfits. It's time to figure out your own personal trademark style. The benefit is that you'll never again buy needless items that don't work with your look or your lifestyle.

Settling on a style allows you to narrow down your purchases. Say you wear classic clothing. Then that bohemian wrap skirt will probably only be wrapped around a hanger in your overstuffed closet. I'm not saying that you can't be influenced by other styles. One day you could feel a little retro and another you might feel more fashion forward. But I'll teach you how to make the most of whatever style you choose on any given day by using the right pieces.

So why pick a style in the first place? You can compare this to a weight-loss system. Maybe you like a diet that's low carb or perhaps you're focusing on cutting fat. The point is that most diets work if you just commit and stick to one . . . but you need an actual plan. If you mix Atkins, Jenny Craig, and the South Beach Diet, you're sabotaging yourself. You're doing a little of this and a little of that. Meanwhile, nothing is actually working. You don't have a formula. Instead, you have a hodgepodge of ideas that don't add up to a workable system. In the same vein, style schizophrenia leads to overshopping, overindulging, and just plain overload because you're trying and buying with wild abandon. No longer will you be a victim of multiple style disorder.

You also don't need to fall prey to whatever the fashion industry is peddling in any given season. If short hemlines are in but you hate your knees, then they aren't for you. We'll find the clothes that highlight your assets and minimize your insecurities. (I'll also offer a few exercises that target and improve some common trouble spots.) But no diet works without working on your attitude. Great style isn't just about picking out the right blouse or boots. Learning to appreciate your own special brand of beauty—including your "flaws"—will help you look better in whatever you wear.

Star Style

Since I've had the good fortune of spending so much time around stylish celebrity figures (and we are all guilty of sometimes living vicariously through them), I thought it would be fun to use these stars as style role models. With your clothing journal in mind, consider which celebrity styles fit the closest to your own unique approach to dressing.

THE CLASSIC: Oprah, Brooke Shields, Michelle Obama, Reese Witherspoon, Kate Winslet, Sandra Bullock, Christie Brinkley

✳ *The Lady*: She knows who she is, and who she isn't. Her innate class, elegance, and timeless poise are never borrowed from a glam squad. It might look like she doesn't take fashion risks, but that's not the case. She simply knows what works for her. She never fails to appear to be anything less than perfect in expressing her unique individuality and personality through her style.

✳ *The Look*: The Classic Look doesn't fall victim to trends. It is clean, unfussy, and completely effortless, as if you had gone shopping in Jackie O's closet. The color palette is black, white, khaki, navy, charcoal, and pastels. Jewelry is never overbearing. Nor does it detract from one's natural sparkle. The shapes and silhouettes borrow from iconic Americana. It's as if the look was pulled from an F. Scott Fitzgerald novel.

✳ *The Pieces*: When cleaning out your closet, be sure to set aside classic white button-down shirts, pencil skirts, sweater sets, shift dresses, simple summer dresses, dark rinse denim, and polo shirts. These will all get a lot of use in your look.

THE ICON: Audrey Hepburn, Grace Kelly, Cate Blanchett, Penelope Cruz, Princess Diana, Madonna, Kate Moss

✳ *The Lady:* Her revolutionary style makes her iconic, and her constant reinterpretation and reinvention keep her relevant. She sets the trends and is utterly fashion forward. Even wearing the uncomplicated, she makes a statement. On her, black doesn't dare to be basic. She is as comfortable in a simple Calvin Klein sheath as she is in a bold Balenciaga ball gown. She doesn't stay with just one look. But if she dares to be caught in the same look twice, she always keeps it fresh with her own special approach and touch. The Icon runs the gamut from simple to bold and brazen, yet never brash.

✳ *The Look:* The Icon is responsible for creating the trend that the rest will follow. She discovers designers and makes them her muse. Grace Kelly gave Hermès the Kelly bag, and Jacqueline Kennedy launched Oleg Cassini into a fashion career with "A Thousand Days of Magic in the White House." Audrey Hepburn sky-rocketed Givenchy into the designer stratosphere. Madonna put Jean Paul Gaultier's cone corsets into the Smithsonian, and Kate Moss single-handedly made vintage ready to wear for the red carpet.

✳ *The Pieces:* Regardless if the item is new or old, you will make it fresh with your signature.

THE TREND ADDICT: Paris Hilton, Lindsay Lohan, Janet Jackson, Nicole Richie, Victoria Beckham, Sarah Jessica Parker

* *The Lady:* She's having a ball. And why shouldn't she? So much to see, so much to do, and she can have it all. This is her mantra. She's always in the mood to try anything new—whether it's a new date, a new BFF, a new restaurant, or a new pair of shoe boots. She's the It Girl Du Jour and her clothing is as current as the name next to hers in the gossip columns.

* *The Look:* Walk through the young designer floor at Saks and Barneys and you will be walking through her wardrobe. Pink and black and sparkles are accentuated by pops of saturated brights, which are as vibrant as her personality. The basic foundation of this look is the accessories—and the more the better. The pieces are in a state of constant flux. They're so up-to-the-minute. There are always some sparkles or rhinestones intertwined. Clothes fit like a second skin—they may be a bit too tight, but that's what makes them oh-so-right. Items and accessories are layered.

* *The Pieces:* In your own closet, watch for key pieces like leggings, oversized tanks, banded mini-skirts, ankle boots, fitted or flirty party dresses, skinny jeans, and cleavage-baring asymmetrical tops. Accessories are over the top, ranging from hardcore hardware like chains and grommets to flirty feminine pieces like ribbons, bows, and flowers.

THE SEX SYMBOL: Beyoncé, Jennifer Lopez, Eva Mendes, Halle Berry, Scarlett Johansson, Kim Cattrall, Raquel Welch, Cameron Diaz

✳ *The Lady:* She's bootylicious, buxom, and boda-cious. Her skin appears as if it were kissed by the sun. When she enters a room, there is a collective, "Wow." Women want to be her and men want to be with her. The boring white T-shirt becomes instantly sexy on her. Jeans seem to melt over her curves. When she steps out in a shorter skirt, pulses race. This girl can't help it. She is sexy, and it shows in everything she wears.

✳ *The Look:* It sizzles, it's scintillating, but it's never trampy. This look is utterly feminine and totally glam-orous. Waists are cinched and outfits are carefully styled to exploit assets and exude the most allure and appeal. Curves are highlighted and flaunted by these vivacious vixens. This look may not be the most practi-cal, but it is utterly luxurious.

✳ *The Pieces:* Heels are a must for the Sex Symbol— in fact, she wouldn't be caught dead without them. Scour your closet for halter tops, fitted corsets, bust-iers, frilly fitted blouses, and tight retro cashmere sweaters, which are all common styles for tops. Pencil skirts with slits, retro capris, and skinny jeans help with asset management on the bottom. Lingerie is a big splurge for Sex Symbols, who favor matching sets in silk, satin, and lace. It's a must to wear sweetheart necklines and anything strapless with '40s and '50s retro silhouettes to hug the curves. Belts are the purrr-fect accessory to cinch this look.

THE REBEL WITH A CAUSE: Angelina Jolie, Demi Moore, Fran Drescher, Drew Barrymore, Sharon Stone

* *The Lady:* Her personality is as passionate as her heart is compassionate. Whether she's assisting with AIDS victims in Africa or glammed up to accept her Golden Globe, her sense of style is impeccable—with an edge. She wears that gown with the daring slit . . . and she just might choose to wear it backward! She mixes Gap tees with couture, showing the world that while she may be concerned with her look, she's much more passionate about her cause than her fashion. By day, she'll be in cargos and an understated piece like the cool leather jacket as she stands in the middle of an orphanage, holding babies to her heart. By evening, she's enjoying dinner with heads of state, bedecked in designer dresses that she wears with subtle nuance. She fits into any altruistic occasion with a vengeance.

* *The Look:* Her style reflects her belief in the power of her choices and her great respect for humanity in all its beauty and pain. She is confident and never pays attention to the critics. She can pull off mixing pieces that most would consider too risky or unapproachable.

She is never afraid of getting down and dirty, but she never leaves dignity behind.

✳ *The Pieces:* For the utilitarian chic-by-day look, pay special attention to those pieces that may have been cluttering your closet for the past decade—like cargo khakis, straight-leg jeans, and leather jackets that make an impact. Contemporary pantsuits, skirts, and blouses are perfect for daytime dress-up and are worn as casually as a pair of pajamas. Black is basic. Color and patterns are used sparingly and just for punctuation. Night is when you can let your feminine wiles run wild. A great black fitted cocktail dress with a dramatic back or asymmetrical neckline is the right touch. And, if it has to be a ball gown, it should be dramatic in its simplicity.

THE MODERN URBAN ECLECTIC: Blake Lively, Rachel Bilson, Gwyneth Paltrow, Joy Bryant, Natalie Portman, Mary Kate Olsen, Ashley Olsen, Jennifer Hudson, Zoë Saldana

✳ *The Lady:* She takes her style cues from the city she lives in and the cities to which she has traveled. She's got a rock 'n' roll edge without being too tough and a feminine side without being too frilly. She never shies away from patterns to express herself, yet she's never overcome by their opulence. No matter what, her outfits always seem like more than the sum of their parts. She gives the same personal panache to simple jeans and a T-shirt as she would to a party dress. There's always something intrinsically "her" about whatever she wears—a subtle quirkiness that makes a statement.

✳ *The Look:* It's all about mixing and matching from different times, places, and styles. It's a bit posh, a bit artsy, and a bit edgy. She subdues her sexy pieces, downplaying the bombshell effect by adding in a little of the Annie Hall factor. It's a mix of heritage and humor by combining vintage pieces from her mother's or grandmother's closet with modern affordable staples from places like Express or Zara. Though she looks like a million bucks, she probably only spent a few. This savvy shopper combs flea markets and Fifth Avenue, stocking up at Saks sales and the Salvation Army to achieve her look. She's an urban shopping huntress.

✳ *The Pieces:* When assessing your own closet, think outside the box. This look is all about combining the unexpected. Edwardian jackets are mixed with modern skinny jeans, while menswear-inspired pieces become daytime attire (tuxedo jackets over tank tops, tailored vests over billowing blouses). Party dresses do double duty as tunic tops. Sexy styles are always layered with vests, cardigans, and tights. Boots, platforms, and extreme heels are common—but never when you expect them. Jewelry is a key tool, usually stacked and multi-stranded (rhinestones are an everyday talisman). Vintage pieces are a must.

THE ROCK 'N' ROLL GIRL: Gwen Stefani, Pink, Rihanna, Fergie, Blondie, Kristen Stewart, Pat Benatar, Cher, Lady Gaga

* *The Lady:* Her vibrant spirit is one of a kind. What flatters her could be ridiculous on the masses—she has an innate disregard for fashion do's and don'ts. Her personal life and career are as colorful as her opinions on everything from politics to food. She's outspoken and entertaining. To put it simply, she rocks. She defies age but never denies it, and she wears that black biker jacket with studs and all—because somehow it always looks right on her.

* *The Look:* It's all about the Cool Factor. But there's a fine line between looking edgy and just plain tough. Balance is the key here—mix the macho metal with some sexy siren. She pairs leather with the vintage cocktail dress, and stilettos or the white tuxedo shirt with the sequin vest. She draws her influences from military, vintage, and a splash of '60s psychedelia. The look is theatrical, without taking it too over the top. She makes her opinions known.

* *The Pieces:* When applying this look to your own closet, keep your skinny jeans, leather jackets, slinky camisoles, stockings (torn or fishnet), and biker boots, as these are the key pieces to this uniform. Mix it up with graphic or message tees, fitted miniskirts, and tailored vests. Leather accents, feathers, or hardcore hardware should be tempered with sparkles, platform

heels, and scarves. Never shy away from spandex, stripes, stars, and plaids—even mix them together. Have fun with accessories, including chains, studs, and fringe. While the color palette may stick to basic black, pop colors of saturated neon pinks and yellows add a striking accent. Top it off with a variety of statement hats, including berets, bowlers, fedoras, and newsboys, to become the consummate performer.

THE HIPPIE PRINCESS: Sienna Miller, Kate Hudson, Ali McGraw, Stevie Nicks, Milla Jovovich, India.Arie, Janis Joplin, Taylor Swift

✳ *The Lady:* She grooves to the beat of her own drummer. Her style and personality are giddy, carefree, and open. One day, it's a paisley peasant top with a velvet vest and Uggs; the next, it's a flowing bohemian vintage floral dress that skims her ankles and reveals her beaded flip-flops. Even when she dons designer duds, they always looks like something she found off a vintage rack. There is nothing ubiquitous about her sense of style. She just lets it be what it will be, man.

✳ *The Look:* Capricious and cute and always a little quirky, this look mixes high and low, vintage and new. Boho chic allows cultures to converge, and our Hippie Princess is truly a citizen of the world. She is an heiress of hip and a goddess of gladiators. This look resists anything with fit. Shapes and silhouettes are as free-spirited as the wearer, allowing both to soar.

* *The Pieces:* This look is fun to interpret since you can always move beyond your own closet for pieces and inspiration without spending a dime. Borrow the earthy jewelry, peasant tops, and prairie skirts from your mother's or grandmother's wardrobe for a more authentic look. Crocheted caps and vests, ethnic-inspired pieces and prints are key. Shearling jackets, wide-leg jeans, and fake fur vests are also essential. Floral tunic dresses, wrap cardigans, and long jersey dresses can be paired with sandals, wooden platform shoes, hobo bags, and satchels. And don't forget the feather accessories.

Food for Thought ⌒

* Make a list of five of your favorite pieces of clothing. Do they fit into any of the previously described star style categories?
* Is there a certain star whose style you like to emulate or whose clothing you pay special attention to when you see her in the magazines? Have you ever clipped out what she was wearing and tried to replicate it? What pieces from your closet would look perfect on her?
* Are you torn between your love of miniskirts (Trend Addict) and your penchant for hippie maxidresses (Hippie Princess)? Do you think you could fit into more than one style category? If so, don't worry, but see if one style is more prevalent than another.

The It Factor

Every once in a while, we meet people whose presence reso-nates a special and captivating quality. It's a spark we find charming. They convey this quality through subtle gestures—touching the shoulder of the person they're talking to, capti-vating people with their quiet, subdued voice, mesmerizing whomever they encounter with their inclusive qualities. There's a little light inside all of us, almost like the pilot light on a stove. I want to make sure you have your light fully turned on, because that ethereal flame is what can turn heads and turn everyone onto you. That is the It Factor. And it fits perfectly into *The Shopping Diet* because it doesn't cost you a dime.

Most of us first encounter the It Factor as kids on the playground, vying for the attention of the leader of the pack. It becomes even more pronounced as we enter high school and begin to deal with the concept of popularity that's epitomized by the cheerleaders, jocks, rebels, and prom royalty. As we learn from these quintessential cool kids, the It Factor is something that is undeniable.

As I matured, I began to understand that the It Factor is an incredibly powerful tool to change how others see and treat us. I really came to appreciate its elusive and beguiling force back in my modeling days. It was the heyday of the single-name supermodel, and Cindy, Claudia, Naomi, and Linda ruled the runways. Carla Bruni (now Bruni-Sarkozy, the First Lady of France) was also a member of the pack. But she was a more subtle beauty and thus never seemed to bask in the same high-profile fashion spotlight as her counterparts. She was gorgeous, but somehow she didn't stand out like those other glamazons.

My opinion of her changed during my first trip to the Cannes Film Festival. I was sitting in a restaurant in St. Tropez, a wide-eyed kid from New York, reveling in the luxury of it all: the beautiful people, expensive food, and sparkling champagne. Suddenly, a hush fell over the aristocratic crowd as a tall, beautiful, fresh-faced girl entered. She was wearing the most understated of outfits in contrast to the diners around her (black bodysuit and leggings, simple diamond stud earrings, plain ballet flats) and her hair was pulled into a sleek ponytail. It was Carla Bruni. Her quiet beauty had quickly taken center stage. Heads turned as everyone watched her walk through the restaurant, hypnotized. This was the moment when I first truly understood the power of the It Factor. It wasn't about what she was wearing or who she was with. It was something inherent within her—an inexplicable glow. I wasn't even sure if she was aware that she possessed it, but to me, Carla epitomized the It Factor at that moment. And as time has told her story, she has clearly made use of it, turning her It Factor into success in modeling, music, and now politics.

While modeling in Europe, another one of my more memorable experiences was having my father come to visit. He was a simple man who worked for IBM all his life. Red-carpet fashion and glamour were way out of his comfort zone. His trip to Paris was a chance for him to see me in my element. I showed him around the city and then brought him to my modeling agency. I briefly parted to check my schedule, and when I returned to the reception area where I had left him, much to my surprise, I discovered my dad surrounded by four handsome models and a very plain and rumpled girl, engaged in conversation. Being my father's son, I couldn't possibly understand why these chic models wanted to talk to him and couldn't even imagine what they were talking about.

As I stood perplexed, the girl turned her face toward me and I gasped. Suddenly, I was pulling my father away by his arm, hoping beyond hope that he hadn't said anything to embarrass me (although it was probably too late for that!). I stuffed us both in the tiny elevator and violently pounded the lobby button. I couldn't get us out of there fast enough. My father was confused: What was the hurry? I said: "Didn't you know who that was?" My father shook his head. "Princess Stephanie of Monaco!" I shouted back. My father gaped. "Princess Grace's daughter?" he asked incredulously. He couldn't believe it. To his generation, Grace Kelly was the personification of style and class. The girl he had just been talking to couldn't possibly be her daughter! Here was a woman who had everything at her fingertips. Poise, dignity, and royalty were literally coursing through her veins. And yet you would never have known it. She was just so regular—no hint whatsoever that she was heir to a throne. Nothing set her apart. She hadn't harnessed her It Factor. And she seemed not to want to. In fact, as time has told her story, she appears to have spent a good part of her life denying and resisting it.

Early in my styling days, I had another memorable run-in with the It Factor. A publicist friend, Karyn Tencer, asked me to meet her new client who was shooting the *Vanity Fair* Hollywood cover with Annie Leibovitz. SmashBox Photo Studios was hopping when we got there. They had combined all three studios into one area larger than several football fields. There were literally walls of shoes, jewelry, and tons of clothing. The room was aglow with beading, sparkles, and lots of glamour. Each star had her own area and glam squad. When I scanned the crowd of Hollywood It Girls, I saw a young woman, her back to me, fixing her dress. As she turned her head, she peered over her shoulder and looked in my direction. The heavens literally opened. She was mesmerizing—her hair shone, her skin glowed, and the sparkle in her eyes was cataclysmic. She dazzled from the inside out, utterly and obviously confident.

Suddenly, Karyn appeared and yanked me over to meet her new client, Jennifer. Lo and behold, the glowing woman across the room was Jennifer Lopez. Unquestionably, JLo is totally in command of her It Factor—she recognizes that she possesses it and she knows how to use it to her advantage. She came from a humble, hardworking background, but she used her It Factor as a catalyst to get her off the block and into the limelight. She's worked it every inch of the way. She has a sense of who she is. And that innate charismatic blend is truly priceless.

These three moments taught me something about the It Factor that I believe is imperative to share with you. Everybody has the ability to possess and command their own It Factor. But the different ways that Carla, Stephanie, and Jennifer have chosen to use their power are what set them apart. Princess Stephanie refused to embrace her It Factor, even though it was hers for the taking. Instead, she ignored its strength. In contrast, JLo recognized and developed her It Factor, harnessing its power to catapult her career from the Bronx to beyond. Carla certainly possessed the It Factor, but it came naturally and truly seemed effortless. She is one of the lucky ones who was simply born with it. Her underestimated and understated use of her It Factor is her greatest success.

Nourishing Your It Factor

You don't need a four-picture movie deal, successful husband, or rich family to have the It Factor. You can be the PTA mom who is always dressed impeccably on her limited budget or the CPA on Wall Street who owns the boardroom with her vibrant personality. Both of these women have the It Factor because they pull it together in their own unique way. There is something that sets them apart. When you possess the It Factor, your style whispers. It doesn't shriek. It follows you and is as alluring as the scent of an unforgettable perfume. People are happy when you arrive and hate to see you leave . . . but love watching you as you go. Do you feel like you are lacking in the It Factor category? Here are some simple things you can do to get some of "It" into your life.

✳ *Opt for less:* Coco Chanel must have had the It Factor in mind when she said this now-famous quote: "When accessorizing, always take off the last thing you put on." These are words to live by from a lady with long-lasting style. Less is more when it comes to the It Factor. Sporting big jewelry, large logos, loud patterns, and brash colors is like screaming when someone is already listening to you. This will only detract from you and your essence. Subtle and slight touches, like the classic sweater, a touch of sequins, or the thin strand of a gold necklace, will accentuate your It Factor. So, if you're ever in doubt, always opt for less. It can say so much more.

✳ *Carry yourself with confidence:* The It Factor is so much more than what you wear; it's the way you carry yourself (and take care of yourself). You can buy any celebrity's sparkling minidress or cell phone—but you can't buy that confidence, that way she strides onto the red carpet or faces a room full of reporters. Even if you aren't feeling confident, the appearance of confidence will take you far. Pull your shoulders back and look people straight in the eye. They won't know that you are feeling insecure. They will simply wonder what your secret is and be in awe.

* *Be kind*: There's nothing more attractive than when you genuinely listen to others with compassion and interest. What gives you the It Factor is being interested and interesting—trust me, your natural beauty will seem to multiply. Talking about yourself and your fabulous possessions will diminish your It Factor. Try to make it about someone else and see the results. Revel in their glow and you'll shine a bit brighter. Offering compliments doesn't cost you anything, but you will be richly rewarded. The It Factor works on the principle of an old Buddhist saying: "A thousand candles can be lit from a single flame and their brightness will never be diminished. Kindness never decreases by being shared."

* *Talk softly*: When it comes to the It Factor, talking just a bit quieter is very alluring. It's an old movie star trick passed down from press offices at the major studios during the '50s. They would instruct their starlets to speak slowly in a hushed tone so that others would lean in, truly listen, and become captivated. The bottom line: Take it down a notch, and the result will be a more classic and classy presentation.

* *Don't dwell on your flaws*: Always bring this truth with you into your shopping experience. The "flaws"

that you dwell on so often will take up less space in your mind if you don't give them the room to reside there. You can lessen their importance by not announcing them to friends or salespeople (e.g., "I hate my thighs"). If someone gives you a compliment on a part of yourself that you think is a flaw, don't argue! Embrace it! You'll soon spend less time hiding what you thought you once disliked so much about yourself and spend more time discovering and accentuating your positives.

Body Beautiful

It's easy to say, "Don't dwell on your flaws." But we all know it isn't easy to accept and even love who you are. That's especially true in our society, which is filled with messages that basically harangue you to find fault with yourself. Even though it's hard, you need to put as much effort into appreciating yourself as you do to tracking the latest fashion trends. And that includes appreciating your body. Then you'll be able to find clothes that look great on you. In order to get started on that big project, you need to first get to know your body.

MIRROR MIRROR

When was the last time you really took a good look at yourself in a full-length mirror? I'm not talking about how you see yourself in your head, but what you really look like objectively from head to toe. Go ahead and take a closer look.

Most people have a completely inaccurate self-perception when it comes to their bodies. The media constantly force-feeds women in particular to think that sizes 2, 4, and 6 are normal. But that's the norm for the *fashion world,* and as we all know, the fashion world is anything but normal. The average female consumer in America is actually size 12–14, so why keep beating yourself up to be something that God never intended you to be or that your lifestyle isn't allowing you to be? If you're not a movie star trying to slip your silhouette into a skinny sample size for an award show, why bother? It's time to embrace the glamour that is you—curves included. After all, those curves are a part of your personal style. *The Shopping Diet* aims to help you become a better, more fulfilled you—not somebody you're not.

Really looking into the mirror is such an important step. As children, we all believe that we're the fairest one of all. But, as we all grow up, we become afraid of the looking glass. So many times, when looking into the mirror, people stop seeing themselves as beautiful and begin focusing on the so-called imperfections. Then they brainwash themselves into thinking the image that they see is the image other people see. I really want to help women make the mirror a safe place again. You need to respect and appreciate every fabulous inch of *you*—the good, and the not so bad. Acceptance is a value that we all have control over. If you dislike your legs and you have been focusing on this repeatedly throughout the years, all the praise in the world is not going to change your image of them. Instead of judging all of your so-called flaws in the mirror, practice nondiscriminating judgment of yourself. You need to accept you, not because of your imperfections, accomplishments, victories, or failures, but because of your inherent worth as a human being. You're going to work with what God gave you and learn how to give it back with a gallon and a half of beauty and glamour.

Take that first step and stand in front of the dreaded mirror—it's really not so bad after all. Now, get down and dirty—take off all your clothes, make sure you're in good lighting (there's no need to torture yourself with fluorescent), and without judgment or any preconceived notions, examine every part of you. I know that for some of you this might be the most emotional and difficult exercise in *The Shopping Diet*. But like our friends at Nike say, "Just do it." You've come this far.

We're all great at picking on the things that we dislike about ourselves, so let's just get that part over with now. List the part(s) of your body that bothers you the most and why.

1. _____

2. _____

3. _____

Ahhhh, that feels better, right? Now, let's move on to the hard part. List the part(s) of your body that you *do* like and why. Don't overanalyze. It could be as easy as your eyes or as simple as your soft skin. For me, it's as little as my mustache—I've been told it's quite dashing!

1. _____

2. _____

3. _____

I think it's clear by now that I'm not asking you to do this exercise for you to feel bad about yourself. I just want you to keep it real and be honest so that you can work on fixing what isn't working for you and embracing what does. And the reality is: Your God-given parts just aren't that bad.

Work with What You Have

So you're standing in front of the mirror and saying, "This is what I am and I am happy." So what if you laugh at yourself? Who said that you have to take every judgment so seriously? (I certainly don't. How could I? I'm a grown man who gets excited and emotional over chiffon and beading!) As we begin to let go of old thought patterns, we make room for new and healthier ones. When you repeat something over and over again for a long period of time, it becomes a belief. How else could you have come to value and believe in your "flaws" over your own beauty? But now you need to believe something new. *You are beautiful.* You need to let go of that negative self-image. Can you do this? Of course you can. Publicists always find something exciting and upbeat to say about their clients. Now, it's your turn. Use the PR spin on yourself by accentuating the positive.

Years ago, I heard about a study in which doctors asked patients suffering from depression to look into the mirror and form a smile, even if they felt unhappy. Those smile muscles triggered their bodies to release endorphins, and if done repeatedly, many patients felt significantly happier over time. They started pretending they were happy and ended up that way. Do this long enough and I bet you will convince even your toughest critic: *you!*

We live with a plethora of media sources. The pages of countless magazines have to be filled with something so that all of us will buy into their limited definition of beauty. Do you realize that these models and stars are real people, too? Half the time, they're stressing and starving themselves to hold onto the images they project. The point is, look at the images, enjoy them, have fun with the myths, but don't get sucked into the idea that this is the way you have to look. These are just ideas and they are here to inspire—not to insult. They're here to help you reach a new level—not to bring you down. The world of fashion is not that serious. It's frivolous and it should be fun—not fanatical.

I recently worked with a company doing makeovers for their annual convention. One of my subjects was a size 22. She panicked at the thought of being seen in a sleeveless dress. So, we compromised with a little black dress with cute cap sleeves, and it was incredibly flattering on her (plus it made her waist look smaller). Yes, her arms were there in full public view. But in her new outfit, she conquered her fears and glided down the runway with the ease of a supermodel. She couldn't stop gushing afterward. Suddenly, she was freed from the burden of trying to hide what she considered a major flaw for so many years. She had never considered that others weren't as focused on her arms as she was. She alone had made them this huge issue. She got many compliments that day. No one came up to her and said, "Wow, we didn't know you had saggy upper arms." Instead, they all talked about how gorgeous and confident she looked. All this time she had been a self-saboteur when, in actuality, all she needed was the transformational experience of a new look and a new way of looking at herself.

I promise you can find that carefree feeling again in the right combination of your old clothes or in a new outfit. It's not about hating your flaws, but working with them to make you see them as fixable or part of a larger, more beautiful whole. Again, you have to identify them first in order to get the ball rolling, and then the love will start flowing. Learning to love yourself is the greatest gift. My career has been about

---

BLOCHBUSTER TIP

For every negative thing you say about yourself, think of three positive things to replace it. It might take some work at first to come up with those replacements, but believe me, it's worth it for your self-esteem and self-image. Hang in there, because it really works.

making the best of things—making a dollar out of 15 cents, a silk purse out of a sow's ear, and a glamour goddess out of a country bumpkin (and no, I'm not naming names). Believe me when I say this is doable.

Solutions for Every Body Type

It's time to divide and conquer. That's my solution for every body type. By breaking the body up into twelve zones and looking at each zone objectively, you will learn how to work with the body that you have—even the parts that you don't care for. You can play certain parts up (by accentuating) or play them down (by camouflaging and making them less obvious), depending on how you feel about each zone. By learning these tricks and keeping them in mind while shopping, you will be able to pick out pieces that complement your favored body zones and redefine the other zones. This process will also help you later face your closet, letting you know which items to keep, which to toss, and which to buy. You are rebuilding your image through choices that are right for *your* body.

HEAD AND NECK

Faces come in many different shapes and sizes: square, oval, circular, and so on. What shape best describes your face? If you have a round face, then I would suggest you buy V-neck shirts and sweaters. If you have a thin, narrow face with a longer neck, then try a turtleneck. An oval face looks amazing

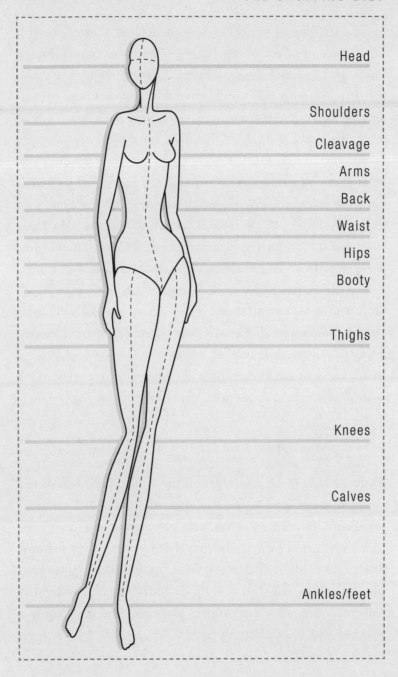

Head

Shoulders

Cleavage

Arms

Back

Waist

Hips

Booty

Thighs

Knees

Calves

Ankles/feet

with a sweetheart neckline. If your neck is shorter, avoid a shirt collar that comes up higher. But if you have a longer neck, you will look good in many different collar styles and heights. You must take complexion and skin tone into consideration as well as eye and hair color, especially when you're choosing clothing shades. Obviously, someone with blue eyes looks great in blues. If you have green eyes, you should highlight them by wearing different shades of green. If your skin tone has colder undertones, stick to tones with the same cool colors. Similarly, if you have a tanned or warmer skin tone, you should opt for the warmer shades. Olive complexions look great in greens and browns. Cooler and less saturated colors like pastel pinks, light lavenders, and soft blues work well with paler complexions. Your haircut, length, and shape are also important elements when choosing the right pieces, especially when it comes to necklines. How you choose to style your hair could directly influence your look—you don't want your clothes, accessories, and hairstyle dueling.

SHOULDERS

Donna Karan made a fortune on the cold shoulder look and deemed it acceptable for millions of women to bear their shoulders. Strapless dresses also have become quite de rigueur on the red carpet. Are your shoulders your best feature? If so, find clothing that plays them up, including halter tops and camisoles that show a little shoulder skin or a piece that falls gracefully off the shoulders. Asymmetrical one-shoulder tops are also an excellent option.

> ## BLOCHBUSTER TIP
>
>
> What you didn't get from the good Lord, you can now buy! One of my favorite tricks of the trade is something we lovingly refer to in the biz as Chicken Cutlets. They are little silicone pads designed to fit into the cup of your bra to give you that extra lift and cleavage enhancement. You can find them at your local department store or Victoria's Secret. They are definitely a part of the "You But Better" philosophy. Why go under a surgeon's knife when you don't have to? Another great trick is to brush some bronzer in between your breasts—this will give the illusion of extra cleavage. And don't forget the iconic push-up bra for a little added oomph. Maidenform's Custom Lift Collection offers a great version as does Wonderbra.

CLEAVAGE

Let's address the age-old question of too much or too little. Of course, it depends if it's shown in the office (show almost none) or out on a date (show some more). The bra is an integral wardrobe component. It's one of the MVPs in a lady's clothing lineup. And honey, those bra straps are meant to be moved! It's crucial to lift and separate; otherwise, what was once at your chest will be down at your waist. So use the strap adjusters on your bra. To all you girls who complain about not being blessed with a bodacious bosom, have no fear! Plunging necklines can be your friend. Go ahead, sport those sweetheart necklines, plunging Vs, and scoop-neck tees. Small breasts look just as good (if not better) in those cleavage-revealing shapes.

ARMS

Few women truly feel their arms are their best asset. If you've managed to be blessed or have worked as hard as an Olympian for some toned guns, you definitely have the right to bear arms! Sleeveless shirts will be for you. Wear those cute little tank tops without worry. If you don't like your armpits to show, try wearing cap sleeves. Even if you don't like your arms, it's not a bad idea to buy tanks and camisoles. Just wear a jacket or a sweater over them. Now more than ever, sleeve lengths are as varied as the climate. The three-quarter sleeve is perfect for those who want to show a little arm but not too much. With the global warming of fashion trends, women are wearing more skin-baring strapless and corseted looks year-round, using blazers, cardigans, or wraps to take these ensembles from work to play.

BACK

Although you might not think about your back much, remember that it's always the last thing seen when you leave. There is something about the sexiness of the curvature of the spine and the softness of a woman's shoulder blades that stays on people's minds. Over the last several years, designers have been doing a lot with illusion backs, cowl drapes, and detailed embroidered or beaded motifs, continually drawing attention to an area that, in the past, many people have taken for granted or have overlooked entirely.

WAIST

The waist should be one of the smallest and smoothest parts of your body. And if it isn't, let's make it look that way. Belts can highlight, accentuate, and even create a feminine shape. If you seem waistless, then you can create one with a looser belt or a chic scarf around your midsection. Using dark colors will make the waist appear smaller. It's crucial to differentiate and separate the waist from the bust. Many people have a high waist, which tends to make the waist and chest appear as one. This gives you a rectangular shape and is less slimming. But if you use a belt to divide and punctuate the space, your waist will miraculously appear. Shapewear is another great solution for creating and defining your waist. Hanes Smooth Illusions or any number of choices from the Spanx line of products work perfectly because they're seamless and will slim you from upper torso to thigh. But my favorite product is the Flexees Waist Nipper, which shapes the tummy and creates a perfect feminine figure.

HIPS

It's great if you have curves like Marilyn Monroe. But beware: Curves can be dangerous. This is another area of the body that is improved and smoothed with the benefits of shapewear. Products like Flexees Boy Short or High-Waist Thigh Slimmer will definitely make you look like you . . . but better. Flowing skirts are great for minimizing larger hips, while pencil skirts are perfect for accentuating them. Again, darker colors are more slimming. Longer tops are a great way to camouflage your curves, especially when the hem of the top falls below midhip, which will help break up your shape. These tops also work if they have a plunging neckline or an empire waist in order to pull the focal point higher on the body. Opt for pants with flat fronts and minimal pockets. (For less bump and bulge, many of my clients often have their tailors remove the pockets from their pants.) Try boot-cut pants or ones with just a little flare. This will balance the curves above.

BOOTY

When Beyoncé's original term "bootylicious" appeared in *Webster's*, we knew that this part of the body was no longer just something to sit upon. This is an area that causes most women to cringe and many men to drool. Even if you choose not to accentuate it, never underestimate the power of the posterior. Comfort is always the key when it comes to the draping dynamics of the derriere. Be careful with jersey fabric, as it can often be far too clingy and accentuate cellulite. Jeans that are too tight should be avoided. Yet, you shouldn't wear pants that are so loose they look like large sacks. A little focus on the booty is a nice touch. A great slim-fitted skirt can sexify the secretarial look. Now more than ever, designers are using fabrics with Lycra. This gives clothing some stretch for increased comfort and flexibility, especially in this hard-to-fit curvaceous zone. If you really want to camouflage your backside, billowing fabrics will hide your booty. Shapewear is another fantastic solution when attempting to downplay the derriere. If your aim is to keep it up and poppin', I suggest products like Flexees Boy Short or Spanx's Power Panty for a little extra lift.

THIGHS

The rise and fall of hemlines has become increasingly tumultuous as fashion's seasons change. Your thighs need room for flexibility. Whether they are thick and powerful or elongated and lean, you must keep in mind your own personal comfort. Microminis, leggings, and hot pants are great looks. But for very muscular thighs, they can be a little overbearing. Instead, try flowing fabrics and camp shorts for summer fun. Wide-leg trousers, A-line dresses, and full skirts are perfect for winter wear. Another multipurpose cover-up is the tunic top. Balloon-cut and empire dresses can do double duty as tops, if they are worn with leggings or slim pants to make a more contemporary statement, which is also flattering to the thighs. Beware of distressed denim that is shaded lighter in the thigh area, which only serves to highlight what you might want to hide.

KNEES

Knees are a difficult zone because there's nothing you can do, exercise-wise, to get them into shape. You either have good ones or you don't. But if you don't have the bee's knees, your legs can still cause a buzz—you might be best suited for pants or tights with different textures and tones (but avoid anything shiny, as this will make legs appear bigger). Ignore the trends and follow your own intuition to pick a hemline that works for you.

CALVES

How you feel about your calves will help determine your wardrobe style. If you like your gams, fill your closet with above-the-knee skirts, cute shorts, and even a miniskirt or two. If you're not comfortable with your legs, go for knee-length skirts and city shorts rather than the Daisy Duke version. Less shapely calves can be deemphasized with knee-high boots, whereas a nude shoe will add more length and emphasis to your legs. If you have larger calves, go for fitted capris that hit halfway between the knee and ankle. Clam diggers look good on thin legs.

ANKLES AND FEET

It may seem like hitting way below the belt to focus on ankles and feet, but we all have our idiosyncrasies. Unless you're born with slim and trim ankles, less is definitely best when it comes to this area. Accentuation of the ankles is all about letting them be. Don't get bogged down with bows and buckles. The gladiator sandal look is probably not for you unless you love your ankles. Instead, elongate the ankle and the silhouette by wearing a flesh-toned shoe or a strappy little sandal, mule, or pump. The shoe boot and the ankle boot can be fashion forward, but they don't work on everyone. Look before you buy, as the style has a tendency to crop and shorten the length of your leg.

Food for Thought ⌒

Now that you've taken a good look at your body objectively, what do you want to highlight? When thinking about the twelve zones, what parts of your body are you proud of— perhaps even taking notice of for the first time? Write down your answers and compare them with your answers in the "Mirror Mirror" section earlier in this chapter.

1. _____

2. _____

3. _____

What part of your body do you want to downplay? Again, write down your answers and compare them with your answers in the "Mirror Mirror" section. You might be surprised by the differences.

1. _____

2. _____

3. _____

Work Out to Improve What You Have

The shape you're in directly affects the clothing you wear. I know this may seem obvious, but we've all seen those girls running around in too-tight clothes. If you're overweight and spending a ton at the stores, then stop for a minute to consider what you're actually doing. Often, when we're caught up in a shopping frenzy and are busy feeling guilty afterward, we don't give ourselves much time to seriously ponder our purchases. One of the main reasons we shop is to feel better about ourselves and how we look. How unhappy we are about our appearance dictates the wicked way we shop. The cost of a nice shirt is generally equivalent to a monthly pass to the gym. At the end of the day, guess which one will leave you happier about how you look and feel? Working out regularly will do more for your appearance than any new outfit. You will end up not only buying fewer things, but also feeling better about the items you already have hanging in your closet. The long-term health benefits are a serious bonus as well. The idea here isn't to change your body. Just be healthy and make the most of what you have.

My friend David Kirsch, a top trainer and founder of Madison Square Club, knows all about getting fit and fabulous. He has sculpted celebrity clients for years, including Heidi Klum, Faith Hill, Ellen Barkin, Kerry Washington, and Linda Evangelista, just to name a few. He was kind enough to offer some great body and exercise tips straight from his workout sessions with the stars.

Q: Do you find that getting in shape affects your clients' shopping habits?

A: Of course, the best part of exercise is getting healthy. But I think a by-product is looking better in clothing. The better my clients look, the better they feel about themselves. Getting in shape means no more hiding in oversized and baggy clothing or buying clothes to try to look thinner, because they *are* thinner.

Q: Is it possible to spot reduce an area of your body?

A: You can absolutely reduce your arms, legs, butt, and abs. You do that with diet and specific spot-reduction exercises. But one word of caution: You just can't say, "I won't eat and I'll lose my belly to fit into that dress or pair of pants." You have to eat right and work out. Genetics, stress, and age also play a part when it comes to stomach fat. But the good news is that you can sculpt sexy arms and lift your ass if it's droopy. You can reduce bloat while losing weight, which will help with abs.

Q: This book is about curbing spending. Do you really need to spend *more* money by joining a gym? If you're strapped for cash, can you get fit without a costly gym membership?

A: My whole philosophy about training is what I call a no-excuse approach to nutrition and exercise. That's why I actually think it's great to work out at home, because it's a friendly and safe environment where you feel comfortable. If you're not structured enough to go to a gym frequently, it doesn't pay to waste money on a membership.

Q: What about the dreaded cardio? I heard that if you work primarily on cardio, then you can lose the weight, especially the belly weight.

A: I don't like to say that you should just get on that boring treadmill. Why not find something fun that you love to do as a cardio exercise? For example, boxing is a very effective cardio exercise because it is constant movement. You're working your legs and arms, while raising your heart rate. Tennis is an amazing cardio exercise. Go Rollerblading or swimming. Get on a bike and race around your town. Just move. It depends on the intensity. The key is to find something you enjoy doing (and no, shopping doesn't count as cardio) so that you will do it often. Go for thirty to forty-five minutes at an intense pace to get more out of it. It's more effective if you're moving and not talking on the phone or fooling around with your Black-Berry.

Q: For clients trying to lose weight, what foods do you advise to nix from their diet?

A: I tell my clients to get rid of the fatty food—it builds up on your stomach. They also should stay away from processed carbs, sugar, alcohol, and all white foods. Forget about diet soda. It's poison and causes bloating. Throw out those cans of diet soda right now.

Q : What if you have an imminent event and need a 911 plan to look good in a gown or in a bathing suit?

A : I have clients who come to me a few days before a beach vacation and say, "I need something to look better in that bikini or in that little miniskirt." I have them do my five-day detox, which is basically eating greens and protein for five days straight. You will lose 100 percent of your belly bloat.

Q : What do you say to the client who wants to drop thirty pounds?

A : The important thing is that you want to do it safely. Take three or four months to lose the weight and stick to a regular plan of diet and exercise. Don't beat yourself up if it takes another month or two to get the body you want. But don't wait.

DAVID'S WORK-ME-OUT TO DRESS-ME-UP TIPS

As celebrity fitness guru David Kirsch says, there are no excuses when it comes to getting in shape. You don't need a fancy gym membership to work out. Here are a few quick at-home exercises proven to get you looking more confident in your clothes.

> * *Upper Body Exercise:* Stand with your legs slightly wider than hip width. Place a medicine ball in front and to the outside of your right foot. Bend from the hips, grabbing the ball, and lift it in a half circle, to the

right, overhead, then to the left. Continue for 30 seconds.

* *Arms Exercise:* Place your tummy on a stability ball and your palms on the floor in front of you. Walk your hands forward as you slide your torso forward on the ball until you come to a push-up position with your thighs, shins, or feet resting on the ball. Note: Stopping with your thighs on the ball is the least challenging option. Place your palms on the floor under your chest. Make sure your abs are tight and your back is flat. Bend your elbows out to the sides as you bring your face and chest toward the floor. Repeat 10–15 times.

* *Legs/Butt Exercise:* Stand facing a sturdy chair. Place your right foot on the chair, then press into your right heel as you extend your right leg and lift your body onto the chair. Step back and try it with your left leg. Don't forget to bend your knees.

* *Calves Exercise:* Flex your calves by standing flat on your feet and then rising up on your toes. Repeat this forty times a day while talking on the phone or brushing your teeth.

All the work you have just done—recognizing which style best represents you and the type of clothing within that style that flatters your body—is crucial preparation for the next important step: the closet cleanse. Step Four is where we take theory into practice by tackling the reality of your wardrobe. Whether you are a Hippie Princess or an Urban Eclectic, the must-have pieces for your look should be the items considered keepers when you start going through your closet. Choosing a style will also make it easier to resist buying new pieces that don't belong in your newly edited and streamlined closet. You'll gain so much by simplifying and figuring out what clothing solutions are relevant to your look and lifestyle.

Not only will you be facing and sorting out the various styles, sizes, and neglected assortment of clothes from your past as you clean out your closet, but you will be learning ways to keep your clothing and clutter manageable, functional, and contained within a space. In this new light, "The Closet" can actually be seen as a very tangible and visual metaphor for your life.

And if you resolve to hit the gym or do your at-home exercises, you just might fit into some of those old clothes you once loved and which we'll unearth during the great closet purge.

part two

Battle *of the* Bulge:

The Closet Cleanse

Step Four:

Reveal the Goods

There's no secret path or password to lead you to your stash of abundance. Just follow the wrinkled, discarded clothing, kicked-off shoes, shopping bags, and boxes. At the end of that cluttered trail, look up—it's *your closet*. Your closet is a reflection of who you are today and exactly how you got to this present moment. If your living room is what you show to the world, your closet is your private diary, a time capsule, and a reflection of who you have been. But even more important, your closet holds the key to the goal of who you want to be. This is the place to gain control over your shopping and spending problems. It's also the mecca for reworking your image from the inside out. You might be shrieking in horror, but trust me, a well-organized, well-stocked closet has more payoffs than just the obvious.

Your closet is one of the first things you interact with every morning and one of the last things you see before you go to bed. In one form or another, you have had a closet throughout your entire life—and it has been with you through thick and thin . . . and whether *you've* been thick or thin! But as you've grown older, your life has become more complicated and so has your closet. When did your priorities change from being a controlled, budget-conscious consumer to needing instant gratification that ultimately created this overstuffed and inaccessible confusion? Well, today your life is going to change in more ways than just having a clean and organized closet.

I know the mere idea of cleaning out your closet sends you running to the couch to watch TV or sip a glass of wine—anything to escape the task at hand. You're thinking it's one of those jobs that can wait until a weekend . . . not this coming weekend, but the weekend after that, or the next? Stop procrastinating! Cleaning out your closet is the *big event* that will finally get your shopping and your life back on track.

The point is not only to clear space to add something new but to showcase what's currently hiding in there. You will be surprised to discover all the beautiful things you already own. Once we make your closet a favorite place to "shop," you will naturally become less tempted to engage in needless buying. After the closet cleansing, you will see the wonder of your wardrobe come back to life in front of your eyes. Separating and banishing the old, outworn, or out-of-date clothing from the must-haves and the treasures will keep you focused on the positive. And isn't that the way you saw your clothes when you first acquired them? It sounds like a fantasy, but the reality is that soon you will be able to open those closet doors and spot the exact skirt or pair of pants that you need *and* that fit, along with a shirt that matches. With the precision of a scanning laser at the checkout counter, you'll cap off the look by zooming in on the perfect pair of shoes. The chaos gone, your racks will look just as desirable and divine as the racks at the highest-priced boutiques. Your closet will become a fabulous little private boutique of its own where you, the buyer, have hand selected every single item and display each with pride.

If all this talk about cleansing has you clutching your bell bottoms from the '70s, saying you can't possibly part with them, relax. We're not going there right now. In Step Four, we will just see what you own by taking inventory. Then we'll talk about the makings of the ideal wardrobe. Wrenching those ragged bell bottoms that no longer fit you from your death grip comes later. . . .

Out of the Closet

It's time to bring your closet's contents out in the open. This might be daunting and a little scary to some, but it's a big step toward your ultimate freedom. With the right attitude, favorite beverage, and inspiring background music, you can even make it fun. But make sure that you are prepared so that there won't be any excuses cropping up at the last minute. Set aside a day when you are not required to do anything else. Don't make any brunch or afternoon plans that create stressful deadlines. This is going to take some time. So carve some out for yourself. Frankly, I think you're worth it.

The first step is to make sure the rest of the room where your closet is located is clean and organized. Make sure you have ample room to pull out all the hidden treasures (and soon-to-be castaways) from your closet. Since the closet is likely in your bedroom, clear off the bed, make some floor space, and empty the trash. You'll need room to work and sort through the clutter. And please wear something comfortable that you can get in and out of easily because you will also want to try on those old outfits with ease.

Gather large garbage bags, stick-on labels, a notebook, a Sharpie, and safety pins. And now is the time to bring in that all-important full-length mirror we worked with earlier. It's one investment that's invaluable when you want to take control of your clothing clutter. It's also a good idea to have a digital camera on hand so that you can take before and after photos of the closet-cleaning process. This is an event that you don't want to forget. More important, keep these photos somewhere accessible so that you can look at them periodically and use them as a reminder to keep your closet in perfect condition.

If your closet is neat and organized, you might be able to evaluate everything without taking clothes off the rods and shelves, but most closets don't get the Good Housekeeping seal of approval. I'm going on the assumption that your closet is a bit of a disaster. And even you neat freaks might pick up a tip about closet maintenance.

The Clothing Pyramid

So now we have arrived at the moment of truth—the *big reveal,* as they say on reality TV. Let's see what you have been hiding in that closet of yours for all these years. Let's take everything out—but not all at once. You don't want to get overwhelmed. I prefer to do it a piece at a time so that you get a good look at what you really have in there.

In my experience with cleaning closets, 99 percent of all people will focus on what they want to keep. In order to make sense of your entire closet, you have to look at the big picture. I know you want to jump to the signature items—the cute little dresses, the shoes with embellishments. The stuff with flair and flash always draws us in. But what about your jeans, suits, and even underwear? You need all those elements for a full-balanced outfit.

Enter the Clothing Pyramid.

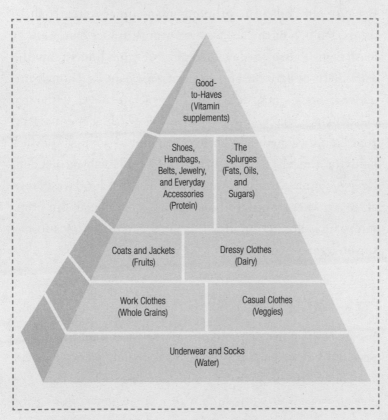

Good-
to-Haves
(Vitamin
supplements)

Shoes,
Handbags,
Belts, Jewelry,
and Everyday
Accessories
(Protein)

The
Splurges
(Fats, Oils,
and
Sugars)

Coats and Jackets
(Fruits)

Dressy Clothes
(Dairy)

Work Clothes
(Whole Grains)

Casual Clothes
(Veggies)

Underwear and Socks
(Water)

The U.S. Food and Drug Administration gave us a user-friendly pyramid, demonstrating balanced nutrition. It puts common-sense eating habits into a visual format that's easy to understand, so there's no excuse for building your diet on fried chicken. You can use the same strategy when it comes to your wardrobe. I've taken the basic format of the food pyramid and applied it to your closet. It reveals what a healthy and balanced closet should look like.

PILE #1 (WATER): Underwear and Socks

Because our bodies are primarily made up of water, you can drink as much of the stuff as you want (in fact, you need at least eight glasses a day to replenish your fluids). It's the same with underwear and hosiery. Stock up on enough underwear, socks, and tights so that you are never without a clean pair (usually about two weeks' worth, depending on your laundry schedule). Throw them out as soon as they get holes or the elastic wears out, and replenish as needed. Keep a couple extra sexy items set aside just for dates! Have at least a week's worth of bras that are wearable and fit properly, which doesn't include any bras where the elastic has surrendered to gravity.

PILE #2 (WHOLE GRAINS): Work Clothes

You need them five days out of the week and want them to be multipurpose and adaptable—just like bread, grains, and rice. You can put rice in a stir-fry or in a pudding. So you should be able to wear your work suits with a great blouse during the day or broken down into sexy separates in the evenings and occasionally on weekends.

PILE #3 (VEGGIES): Casual Clothes

Think of this category as the fuel to maximize your movements. This includes your favorite jeans, casual T-shirts, and whatever else you wear during your off-hours and on the weekends. Make a large pile of all of your "play" clothes. Include the items that aren't good enough for work or social events but are fine for casual time at home or with the family. We will later eliminate what you don't need from this pile. Remember that having it all doesn't mean keeping it all.

PILE #4 (FRUITS): Coats and Jackets

Like two servings of fruit per day, you really only need two sorts of outerwear: fancy and casual. Remember, fruits are high on carbs and natural sugars, which take up a lot of room in your caloric diet. Likewise, coats and jackets take up a ton of space, so it's a good thing to get them out of the closet and examine the ones that still work. Ideally, you should keep your coats out of your clothes closet and put them in a closet closer to your front door. I imagine that you might have coats that are so old or odd that you would never dream of wearing them again. Set them aside, but don't throw them out. In most cold-weather cities there is a severe need for outerwear. Your old puffy jacket might make someone who's less fortunate a lot warmer and happier.

PILE #5 (DAIRY): Dressy Clothes

You don't want too much cream in your diet, but you want to have *some* richness. Man cannot live by whole foods alone. These are the little black dresses, fancy suits, and other clothes that serve as your special events clothing. This pile consists of all the clothing you reach for when heading out for a night on the town, a date, or a trip to the theater. (Don't confuse these with work clothes, which should be more subdued.) Be sure to add any special occasion clothing (especially any that you may have only worn once) to this pile. This includes that peach-colored bridesmaid dress from 1982. We will discuss how to reinvent items in Step Six.

PILE #6 (PROTEIN): Shoes, Handbags, Belts, Jewelry, and Everyday Accessories

Just as meat can make your entrée tasty, your accessories can do the same for an outfit. It's important to keep quantity in mind. You wouldn't want too much meat, so don't wear too many accessories. Make subpiles for each accessory category (put all the jewelry in one area, the handbags in another, and so on). Make sure that all accessories are included, and don't forget scarves, earmuffs, and even that crazy hat you bought at the flea market on a whim. Since many of us have a closet worth of shoes alone, it's helpful to divide the shoe pile into minipiles that include dressy, casual, sandals, and boots.

PILE #7 (FATS AND SUGARS): The Splurges

These are the Jimmy Choo's, Prada handbags, perfect Marc Jacobs dress, and Gucci sunglasses that you bought for . . . okay, we won't even whisper the amount. These items are near the top of the pyramid because you shouldn't have an entire closet of splurges. Treat your high-priced treasures with care by making sure you pile them on a soft and special spot like your down comforter. They are *investments,* and it's time to give them some breathing space so that they will last for years to come. This doesn't mean preserving them like museum pieces. I want you to use them instead of just saving them for a special occasion. One sentence I hate to hear is, "I'm saving this for something special." Nobody is promised tomorrow. Make every day special. Take your splurge out of its wrapper, wear it, and enjoy it!

PILE #8 (VITAMIN SUPPLEMENTS): The Good-to-Haves

This pile includes workout clothes, PJs, robes, and bathing suits. These specialized items supplement your wardrobe and don't belong in any other pile.

PILE #9 (TRANS FAT, HIGH-FRUCTOSE CORN SYRUP, AND FOOD COLORING): All of the Other Stuff Lurking in Your Closet

I know people who have paintings, stuffed animals, gifts from old boyfriends, and CDs in their closets. Just like unhealthy food additives, you need to get rid of them! If it's at all possible, remove the nonclothing items, store them elsewhere, give them away, donate them, or just toss them. They're creating eyesore clutter that is stopping you from recognizing what's good in your closet.

∽

You are sitting in your bedroom with piles all around you, probably thinking, *What the heck did Phillip get me into?* However, you are starting to get a picture of your wardrobe as it is. The casual clothes pile might be more like a mountain, whereas your work clothes pile has only two out-of-date suits. Don't worry. We are going to get your Clothing Pyramid into shape.

In Step Five, we are going to take your piles and make even more piles. That's right. We are going to sort through each category to figure out what to keep and what to ditch. Just as we are getting rid of excess spending and debt, we're also losing the bad purchases that have been causing your closet quagmire. Once you know (and like) what you have in your closet, you'll effortlessly get out of your fashion rut. You will no longer instantly grab your go-to outfit—an old T-shirt and jeans—because you don't want to disrupt the beast.

As you go into the next step, think less is more. Ten great pieces in your closet that you actually love and wear trump fifty items that you don't wear and are just on display in the Museum of Clothing Past. Come to terms with the fact that what came out of your closet isn't necessarily going back in. We are going to take a hard and honest look at what items work with your style, your body, your spirit—and what to do with the stuff that doesn't pass the test. Be brave!

Step Five:

Ditch What Doesn't Work

There is no single formula that applies to everybody when it comes to what to keep and what to eliminate as you clean your closet. It depends on a person's lifestyle, individual look, and current body type. Chances are what you like and don't like about fashion have changed over the years. And whether you like it or not, so has your body. Maturing means your preferences and opinions change and evolve. Another part of growing up is making more appropriate decisions based on the changes in your life. So ask yourself, "How many midriff-baring camisoles do I really need?" That look may still work for Madonna, but I bet this material girl probably needs more material now. Ask yourself, "How many pairs of low-rise jeans should I own now that I've moved from college to a career?" Those torn patchwork Levi's will definitely not make the grade if you try to take them from classroom to boardroom.

I want you to reprogram your mind to make smart decisions about what fits on your body and in your life. Let's go back to the jeans: When it comes to denim, consider keeping a pair that is formal and a pair that is more comfortable. In my closet, I have a personal pair that I like to kick around in and a presentable pair that I can wear out in public. You also may need a light-colored pair and a dark-colored pair. As jean trends change so often these days, you might want to hold onto a skinny style and a wide-leg style.

It's not about trends; it's about style. Don't keep a trend because it's "in"; keep it because it works for you. You can have several styles or versions of any given item. For instance, it's fine to have three different black blazers as long as they are not the same style. Different brands or labels from diverse seasons will give you a variety in their interpretation of the same item. If one is cropped, one is oversized, and one is fitted, you're set. Remember, we are looking for variety and outfit options.

Okay, it's decision time now. You can do it. And I'm here to help you remain consistent through the process. Do those pants give you a muffin top? Bye-bye. Which pants give you the hot butt? Hello. Do you have items with the tags still on them? Return them if it's not too late. Even store credit is better than a stack of clothing you will never wear. If you have the space to keep clothing that you love but doesn't fit, store these items in a place other than your main wardrobe closet. They can be good motivators to get you back into your former size. However, you don't need a whole other wardrobe as a kick in the butt to slim down—just keep a few of the more exceptional pieces. But if you lack the archive space, they have to go. And if your closet is cluttered with shoes that you love but are uncomfortable, get rid of them or donate them—they are not going to get more comfortable over time. Nothing uncomfortable or unused should take up valuable space in your closet. I'm a big believer in shopping karma: If you give away a pair of shoes, something better will come.

Start thinking of your closet as the most important area in your home—it is, after all, the area where you house the items that you use to present yourself to the world. Remember, your closet is a functional place and should have flow: The pieces should come out to be worn and then returned to their place. No item should stay stagnant. The goal is to keep clothing, accessories, and shoes on a constant rotation. Anything that doesn't make it into the cycle doesn't make the cut.

BLOCHBUSTER TIP

I want you to apply three questions to all the clothing in your piles: How does this fit in my life? How does this fit on my body? How does this fit in with my personal style? It's a process I like to call Fashion Fanatics Mathematics, and it adds up for any item.

Decisions, Decisions, Decisions

Figuring out what to keep can be an emotional step for many people. A good way to start this process is to refer back to your clothing journal in Step Two where you wrote down everything that you wore for two weeks. We are going

PHILLIP BLOCH

to revisit your piles (casual clothes, accessories, splurges, etc.) and break them down into even smaller piles of the following categories: keepers, fixers, returns, items to sell, giveaways, and throwaways. Once we are done with this process, it will be undeniably clear what's returning to your closet.

THE KEEPERS

These are the clothes that you love and wouldn't consider getting rid of under any circumstances. You will put this pile together on impulse the first time you visit it. But once you have set your emotions aside, take a second look at these items and make sure you're not just attached to them on an emotional level. You just can't love an item for the idea of it (or because you wore it when you first met your boyfriend). By now you have learned to consider what the piece does for your body and your lifestyle. If it makes your hips look smaller, or you can wear it with pants to a meeting or add an embellishment or accessory to make it work at a banquet, then knock yourself out. Ask yourself the following questions before putting an item into the keeper pile.

* Have I worn this item within the past year?
* Does the color and/or cut bring out the best in me?
* Is the item comfortable enough to wear for hours?
* Does this item make me look good? Or does it make me look *better*?
* Do I feel good in the item? Or am I constantly fussing and fidgeting with it?

* Is this piece transformational? Can I get several uses out of it (e.g., could I wear it during the day, at night, at the office, on the weekend)?

* How does it fit into my clothing journal in Step Two?

* Do I want to keep this item or just the story that is attached to it?

* And last but not least, do I *love* it or do I just like it?

The reasoning behind these questions is based on sense and sensibility and not emotion to help make up your mind. You just can't love the item for the idea of it.

BLOCHBUSTER TIP

You may need evidence for why you need to keep a piece or why it should be sentenced to the donation bin. Put the item on trial together with different pieces, accessories, and shoes to create at least three new looks. Then photograph yourself in those looks. These photos will become evidence (Exhibits A, B, and C) in favor of the item. If you can work it in well with different pieces, then you have found several new outfits! Put the successful looks into a clothing photo album that you will stash in your closet and refer to later for inspiration when getting dressed.

THE FIXERS

These pieces have stains, unraveled threads, scuffs, or worn elastics. They're the items that are more distressed than Barack Obama's first year in office. In fact, these are probably some of your favorite go-to pieces, since they have been worn so much they are at the point of disintegrating. Unfortunately, at this point, every time you grab for them, you think, *Ugh! I can't wear this because it's got that makeup stain on the collar. I've got to fix that!* And then you put it back in the closet. These favorite items remain unfixed in your closet's confines for weeks, months, even years. Many people just want to toss these items in the garbage bin out of frustration, but listen to your stylist: Don't jump to the dump. It's often easy to fix what's broken, and you can add years to an otherwise wonderful piece. Fixing is a great way to save some money. It doesn't take much more time and effort than a trip to the tailor or dry cleaner. Here's what you need to know about these two important services.

* *A Good Tailor:* I always like to test a few tailors out before I commit to one by giving them each a similar item of clothing (e.g., a dress that needs to be taken in) and seeing who finishes the job the fastest, who charges the least, and most important, who does the best job. Quality is key—a bad tailor can make expensive clothes look cheap, whereas a good one can make inexpensive clothes look like couture.

* *A Trusty Dry Cleaner:* Too many times we spend money on dry cleaning that is barely passable. As with

the tailors, check them out beforehand by taking similar pieces of clothing to several of them. Always make friends with the clerks at the desk, because you will get better service and can come to them if there is a problem. Through time, they will understand your needs and will go that extra mile for you. For special high-ticket items like a leather jacket or a couture gown, I always work with a specialized dry cleaner in New York named Madame Paulette (www.madame paulette.com). They guarantee their work and accept items from all over the world. And while they definitely charge more, sometimes for the finer things in life you get what you pay for.

THE RETURN PILE

This pile is for any pieces in your closet that you haven't worn and still have the original sales tags on them. If you miraculously still have the receipt, most department stores will accept a return and give you full credit. Boutiques may have stricter policies. If you *don't* have the receipt, usually you can still take the item back and be issued a store credit. But if the item has been marked down since your purchase, you will only be given the final markdown price. So, if you originally purchased the item for $75 and the final markdown price is $10, that's the total you'll receive. That's why, if you don't already, you should keep all your receipts in a convenient place, such as in an envelope or a designated drawer or box. Don't just throw the receipt in your purse or keep it in the shopping bag. You know that filing system has never worked.

BLOCHBUSTER TIP

Don't forget the possibility of having a fantastic garage or yard sale, on your own or with a friend, to get rid of the items you no longer need. It's a great way to meet the neighbors, make extra room in your closet, and make a little extra cash. Afterward, treat yourself to a night on the town or use the money to pay off some credit card debt.

THE "SELL IT, SISTAH" PILE

You can make some money by selling items you no longer want at a consignment shop or on eBay. (There are even companies that will take your items and put them on eBay for you in exchange for a fee or percentage of the sale.) You can get a better price for an item if the original price tags are still attached. It's often worth the trouble of selling a piece of clothing, even if you can't imagine anyone else buying it. You might think that Michael Kors blouse from several seasons ago is worthless, but someone out there may be willing to pay a pretty penny for it. What do you have to lose?

THE GIVEAWAYS

I love the idea of giving clothing where it is needed or wanted. If one of your friends loves the color blue, be a true blue friend and set aside that aqua cashmere sweater you haven't worn in years for her. If your sister has always coveted that beaded vest, now's the time to make her day. Maybe you have a friend who isn't as fashion fortunate as you or has a new job and can't afford to buy something fresh for the office. Remember that one person's castoff is another person's couture, so give her those unworn office separates. And if you dry clean the item first, it makes an even better gift.

It's thoughtful to give clothes to friends and family, but it's downright uplifting to donate them to charities or a shelter. Some people who are trying to get back on their feet don't have the necessary wardrobe basics to interview for jobs. Your excess bags, dresses, shoes, and accessories could be the perfect touch to help someone less fortunate dress to impress and get hired.

BLOCHBUSTER TIP

One great idea is to have a swap-meet party with friends who are also in the same clothing overload predicament as you. Set aside one weekend where you will each clean out your closets and then bring all your extras to one friend's garage or basement. Go through each other's items and see if there's anything you would like to trade. Don't take clothes just because they are free. They have to look good on you and fit in with your lifestyle. Otherwise, you'll end up with a closet filled with another set of clothes you never wear.

BYE-BYE FAT CLOTHES

If you've lost weight, now is the time to reward yourself by taking all those large clothing items and splitting them up among consignment, giveaways to friends, and charity. Don't leave the high sizes in your closet as an open invitation to slip back into bad eating habits. You don't want to sort through those old pants and shirts from your past when you get dressed in the morning. It's time to live in your new gorgeous present. Not having the clothing available and knowing that you will have to go out and buy bigger sizes again is the best way to stick to your new healthy diet or exercise plan.

THE THROWAWAYS

This, hopefully, small pile is for the *junk* that just needs to be put out of its misery because it's beyond repair and frankly no one should be asked to wear it. Grab a big trash bag and fill'er up. But remember, this should be your last-resort pile, because giving away is far better (and greener) than throwing things in the Dumpster.

Don't Delay

Here is where your labels and Sharpies come into play. Label each bag with its destination. For those bags bound for the consignment store, first and foremost, make a printed list of everything you are consigning. Make one copy to give to the store and keep another copy for yourself. Then, to make life easier, put items together with their kind—keep shirts with shirts, dresses with dresses, and so on. This will make the check-in process at the consignment store smoother and more successful. Before you try to sell anything, make sure you have detailed instructions about how the consignment store operates. Sometimes they will not take items that are not in season or they find unacceptable for some reason. Anything refused should be immediately added to the donation bags. Otherwise, it could sneak back into your closet.

For items to be donated, there are two kinds of charities: organizations where your clothes will be redistributed to those in need or places where your clothing will be sold so that the proceeds can go toward a specific cause. Regardless of which you choose, remember to get a receipt. You can write these donations off on your taxes.

The most expedient way to get these bags out of the house and out of your life is to put them right by the front door so that they're staring you in the face every time you come and go. Or better yet, just put them in the car right now. The longer you let the bags sit by the door or in your car, the longer you will deny closure on the closet cleansing (and the greater the chance of those items sneaking back into your closet). You've worked hard to get to this point. Don't let inertia negate all that great sorting and sifting.

This is the point in the closet-cleaning process where people start getting a little depressed. It is the drop after the positive adrenaline rush. When you first brought all your clothes out into the open and revealed an empty closet filled with possibilities, it felt great. *(Wow, I didn't realize how much space and clothes I have.)* But now the reality of your piles is settling in. Maybe the keepers pile is small and the giveaway one is huge. Staring at the fix-it pile, you are overwhelmed with memories—you had lots of great moments in those clothes, some of which are worn beyond repair. But you aren't ready to part with them for sentimental or financial reasons. (Hey, you spent a lot of money on that stuff!) Well, have no fear. Step Six is all about giving those old clothes a new life.

Step Six:

Reinvent the Favorites

In Step Five, we divided your closet's contents into piles, one of which was the fix-it pile. Step Six focuses on this particular pile of items that have seen better days but which you still aren't willing to donate, sell, or throw away. As you revisit this pile, start to use your imagination to figure out something creative to do with the pieces. Sometimes it's about altering an outfit with quick and easy solutions, such as changing the buttons of a blouse or taking the sleeves off a sweater. You can turn clothes that are past the point of repair into something entirely different—like a pillow or costume. I'm not advocating you become a pack rat. Certain things like old underwear with no elastic need to be tossed. But if you simply can't part with a sentimental item, it's better to transform it than have it taking up space in the back of your closet.

You might want to jot down your ideas in your notebook as you sort through the items—the creative mind can overflow and it's hard to remember all the brilliant plans you come up with. And don't censor yourself, no matter how far-fetched your ideas may seem. A talented tailor can do tricks you'd never believe possible. Set aside a bag labeled "Tailor" for the jobs you think are too complicated to tackle yourself and another marked "Fixers" for DIY projects. I always find it helpful to write down an expiration date (aka: the date I want the projects finished). Don't give yourself more than a month; otherwise, these bags will just move around and around until they orbit back into your closet. And we've come too far forward to regress now. Keep the "Fixers" bag in plain sight. You'll be more apt to work on the items while watching TV or relaxing if they're right in front of you. The image of that big plastic bag messing up your living room decor will be motivation enough to get started and get done.

Fantastic Fixes

A big part of a stylist's job is to figure out the fixes that will make an outfit perfect. It can be as simple as a small nip to the waist of a pair of pants that a client otherwise loves. Or it can be a last-minute repair to a broken zipper of a gown right before a star makes her grand entrance onto the red carpet. Think McGyver to the fashionista. Here are some of the best tricks I have up my chic sleeve to fix your own fashion problems.

THE FRAY

If you have a top that's a bit frayed around the edges, a gros-grain or velvet ribbon can be the perfect cover-up when sewn on top of those ragged seams. Try a contrasting color for a little extra pop. Ribbon is a great trim to use as an addition to a preexisting piece of clothing in order to create a brand-new piece or to dress up an item that was originally too plain and simple.

FIT TO BE TIED

Give a shirt whose once-tight elastic cuffs are now sagging new life by replacing the elastic in question. If you're handy with a needle and thread, a more creative way to solve the problem is by removing and replacing the elastic with a thin satin or velvet ribbon that you can then tie into a beautiful bow. This solution works for long- and short-sleeve shirts.

REPEAT OFFENDER

You might have a gown that's so gorgeous (and expensive) you've worn it at least a dozen different times—so many, in fact, that your friends and family members can instantly spot you at any event. It's time to reinvent this beauty by cutting it off! And I don't mean just making it into a shorter dress. Cut this one off at the waist. First, try the dress on. Find the appropriate length (leaving a little extra for hem or waistband) and snip, snip, snip. This is a great idea for halter-top dresses. Suddenly, one gown or dress has multiplied into two great separates, a top and a skirt: two brand-new pieces with a lot more versatility in a color and fabric that you already know you love.

SMART ADDITION

To remake a skirt or dress that seems out of style or overused, add a different fabric or trim to the bottom or even add a ruffle at the hem. A skirt or dress that may have been too short before takes on a whole new look (and length). If you have a strapless dress or top that you're bored with, add a strap made from a beautiful ribbon or piece of lace. For a touch of sparkle, use a strand of rhinestones or beading, which you can purchase premade at a notions or fabric store.

CUFF IT

Cuffs are the first thing to get ruined or dirty on a shirt. Take an old blouse, making sure there are no irreparable stains on it first, and cover any rip or tear in the cuff seam with some gorgeous black satin piping or ribbon. Sewing piping onto anything is tricky. You have to make sure you know the craft of undersewing so that the stitches won't show. If you have any doubts, take the item to the tailor. If your cuffs are beyond repair but the body of your shirt is still in good shape, replace them. For a very fashion-forward touch, switch out the cuff color to contrast the shirt. Go for faux fur on your coat cuffs or collar for a fancy and fun fall/winter adjustment.

ALL BUTTONED UP

Revive an old blouse by taking off its buttons and replacing them with ornate ones. You can find some unusual buttons at secondhand stores. Usually, they have a big assortment all bunched together, so it may be hard to find the exact number of one type of button that you love. But sometimes you can hit the jackpot. And why does everything have to be so matchy-matchy? Each button on your shirt can make its own little fashion statement. Just make sure the buttons are the same size and that they will fit in the existing buttonholes.

ARMS CONTROL

If you have a fabulous blouse or dress but a sleeve is ruined with a stain, rip, or moth holes, just have the sleeves removed! You don't have to be Michelle Obama to go sleeveless. You can create the perfect sleeveless shell for summer and then take it into the fall and winter season by wearing it under a jacket or cardigan.

SHIP SHAPE

A great way to turn any white, navy, or black piece into something with a nautical edge is to change out the buttons for new ones that are big, bold, and gold. You could even add gold braiding or rope for a fun trim. Your piece won't feel like the same Old Navy item—this is the new military style!

TRAIL BLAZER

Don't toss that wide-lapelled, too-long, and out-of-style blazer! With a little love, care, and repair, we can make this something you'll want to wear. Reduce the width of the lapel and, for a little extra touch, switch out the lining for a contrasting color or pattern. Or take a walk on the wild side and use a tasteful animal print. This is an exceptionally fun take if you roll and cuff the sleeves to three-quarter length so that the new lining gives your outfit a little extra pop for everyone to see. Hem the blazer to the length you like and that works best for your body—perhaps even a shorter cropped length that's more modern. When finding the hemline that's right for you, always think about camouflaging your hips. Any extra fabric removed from the hemline can make a fabulous belt to draw attention and add definition to your waist.

THE LAW OF PROPORTIONS

It's much easier to slim down a dress or skirt that is too big than to make the same pieces bigger. So that dress you always wore when you were overweight can transform with the use of some sartorial skills from a size 16 to a size 6. Keep this in mind when shopping for bargains. If you find a fantastic steal that's a little too small, it might cost you a fortune at the tailor's to fix it. Better to stick to your size or a little bit bigger.

BE DAZZLING

It's the holiday season and you need something new to wear with that low-cut top besides the same old pair of black trousers you've worn for the past two seasons. Go to the fabric store and get a strip of rhinestones (not too thick) and sew them down the outside seam on each pant leg for a fun play on the traditional tuxedo pant. It's a great way to be dazzling.

STAIN FIGHTER

An important warning for protecting your clothes and saving on dry-cleaning dollars: Always test perfumes, deodorants, creams, and ointments to make sure they will not have an adverse chemical reaction on various fabrics. Certain liquids and creams, particularly ones used as medication, have a tendency to irreversibly stain, bleach, or ruin clothing, especially when perspiration is involved. So do your research, read labels, and test lotions and potions first on a nonvisible area on old clothes. To be extra safe, wear a cotton T-shirt as a barrier between your skin and the garment in question.

FANCY FEET

Shoes can be repaired easily by adding a new outer and inner sole, balancing the heels, stretching them, dyeing, or polishing. If you have a pair of shoes that you consider boring, think about what you can do to jazz them up. You can buy buckles and have the shoe repair person sew them on, or have textured leather sewn on as a trim or an accent (this is a great solution for hiding a scuff or rip). But don't hang onto these shoes trying to come up with ideas. That lightbulb will never come on in a year if it doesn't come on now. Donate if you can't think of a creative transformation.

Get Crafty

Our *Shopping Diet* pursuit to save money isn't just about curbing your shopping impulse by reinventing the clothes you already have in your closet into fabulous new looks. There are plenty of opportunities to use those closet-hogging items for purposes other than outfits. There are tons of things that are cluttering up your closet that you can transform, recycle, and reinvent with a little imagination and skill. If you have a sewing machine, a quick trip and a couple of dollars at the arts-and-crafts store can open up a whole new world of fun and crafty activities for you. But don't keep these items in your clothing closet. Keep them where you can get at them easily—a family room or playroom closet is my best suggestion, as this is where these items will actually get used. Here are some ingenious ideas that might surprise you.

* Perhaps you have an old full-length slip that your grandmother wore in the '40s, but it hasn't fit you since the '90s. It is now looking pretty pitiful and tattered, having languished on that wire hanger for so long. Now it is time to use your imagination. Let's take the beautiful hand-embroidered lace from the hem

and make it into curtain ties. Let's take the supple silk fabric from the body of the slip and turn it into a showpiece pillowcase. You can use an old throw pillow as the base for this. If you don't have a sewing machine or you lack the time to do this yourself, you can take all of the materials to the tailor.

✳ I spent a day with my friend and client, Christie Brinkley, organizing her closet. She is an extremely creative and artistic person, so we tossed around ideas about reinventing her old favorites. Her main focus is on her children, so she is totally into arts and crafts. Christie invents Halloween costumes for her children (and herself) from items in her closet that are no longer red-carpet ready. Why go out and purchase a new Halloween costume every year? You can save money and create family fun by inventing your own. And the costume is guaranteed to be unique! How about that old trench coat that has been hanging in the closet since the great flood? To turn it into your costume for the next office Halloween party or join your kids in trick-or-treating fun, all you need is a pipe, funky hat, and magnifying glass (available at a secondhand or antiques store) and, pronto, you're Sherlock Holmes for a mere pittance. How about that old black town gown? Think about it before putting it in the donation pile. Get some long opera gloves, a cigarette holder, faux pearls, a pair of sunglasses, and an accent and, presto, you're Audrey Hepburn.

✳ Do you remember when you bought that souvenir shirt twelve years ago? That was a trip that holds many fine memories, but that shirt won't even go over your head now. Why not cut out the main pattern or graphic from the shirt and frame it? Wearable art becomes living room art!

✳ If you're hanging onto bags full of baby clothing from your children, who are now out of college and on their own, buy some plain, wide, inexpensive picture frames and cover them with that great little cowboy print shirt or the lace from the pink ballerina tutu. Stretch the fabric out across the frame and glue gun it to the back. Then put your favorite baby pictures in the frames. This concept also works for sequined or beaded fabric remnants from evening wear past. You can cover plain storage boxes in these fabrics as well, making them a decorative place to keep photos and other mementos.

As you can clearly see, there is an endless list of possibilities for reinventing old favorites. You just have to make the time, put in the effort, and let your imagination run wild. Now the task at hand is to find the space to return all those items you've fixed (as well as all your nice and neat piles of various types of clothing) to the closet.

You should be amazed at how far you've come. You now have the blueprint for your fashionable future. This is the basis for a wonderful and workable wardrobe. As we put everything back, we want to keep things in a very organized manner for efficient use. That drive to organize will be infectious and will spread throughout your entire life. You will know where everything is, since all items will be in their allocated space. Your new closet will save you time by allowing you to immediately find the article you are looking for. It will save you money by knowing what you have so that you don't purchase similar items over and over again. You will rejoice at the outcome on a daily basis. But first, we have to get organized.

Step Seven:

Reorganize Your Space

Most people don't use their closet space well. As they buy new shirts or shoes, they just move the older stuff aside in an effort to make more room. It's a constant game of push and shove. There's little thought as to how to ensure your clothes are easily visible and accessible. Here's one of the most important secrets to looking great: You need to actually see all the clothes you own. That's because it's easier to visualize outfits if you can see all your options.

You've spent a lot of time organizing your clothes. Now let's organize the space where they'll live. You need to analyze every nook and cranny of your closet (leave no inch unused!) and think hard about what you own and how it best fits into the space you have. You might also have to put on a tool belt and take a trip to your local hardware store. It will be worth the effort after you witness the glorious temple dedicated to your personal style. Once you have redesigned your closet's interior—adding any new shelves, storage units, or hanging rods that are helpful—I will give you tips on how to best organize your clothing, shoes, and accessories within the new design. The result will be the best boutique you've ever seen!

Closet Makeover

You aren't the only one who is going to look more gorgeous after undergoing *The Shopping Diet*. Your closet is about to get a makeover, too. You don't need to call in some fancy closet company for interior track lighting or any other unnecessary bells and whistles. This is about putting the function back into your closet. And you can do that yourself and save money. Start by taking an exact measurement of the width and height of your closet as well as the dimensions of its interior in order to truly understand what items you can fit back into it and how. Consider and assess any shelf, storage, or rod additions you will need based on the type and amount of items that you are putting back into your closet. (Look at your piles as a guide.) Calculate how many hangers you will need as well as how much space your itemized piles of folded clothes will need. If you don't have the skills to make these additions happen painlessly, definitely ask (or pay) someone to help you. But the design of your closet should be based solely on your storage needs and what will be most practical and efficient for you on a daily basis.

MAKE A SKETCH

To understand your closet space better, use your notebook to sketch the space (use graph paper or a ruler if this helps). The drawing should include any shelving and rods that are already in it. You don't have to be Picasso! We don't want to get too technical here for those who have very little skill in carpentry or who don't want to spend the money on a closet makeover company. Drawing out a plan, no matter how simple your sketch is, will force you to think concretely about the space and its proportions. It will act as a helpful guide when you go shopping for storage units and closet accessories.

CONSTRUCTION IDEAS

Look at the construction of your closet to see if you're using all the available space. Most of the time, you can add another shelf above your highest shelf to store shoes or sweaters that are not in season. Make sure this space is easy to get to and easy to view. A small stepladder or footstool that is easily accessible can make your closet a more functional and efficient space. Think of your closet as a giant stage. And you want to be able to see everything that's happening at once.

Consider enlarging the opening to your closet, possibly making the doors span from floor to ceiling. As the entry walls surrounding a closet are usually not structural, this is an easy fix that any handyman can do, and it won't cost you a lot of money. I gained several extra feet of storage by enlarging my own closet entrances. And interestingly enough, this enlargement will make the rest of your room look bigger because of the strong vertical lines it creates architecturally.

SPRUCE UP THE INTERIOR

If the walls of your closet are trashed with scuff marks and have chips of drywall missing, it's a good idea to clean them up while you are doing this major overhaul. Repair the drywall. (You can get drywall repair kits at any hardware store.) Follow up by painting the closet interior—with quick-drying paint—in a light color that matches the walls of the room the closet is in. That is an elegant touch to add to its brand-new look and appeal.

GO SHOPPING

I suggest you go to a one-stop shop like Home Depot to get any shelving, storage, and hardware you think you will need. At this point, it's better to buy more and return what you don't need when the job is done in order to save yourself multiple trips to the store. Just make sure to check on the return policy of each store and save your receipts religiously.

Ask for closet-organizing diagrams at these chain hardware stores or ask an employee to help you get started if you need a hand. Believe me, they do this kind of thing all day and know how to get the job done. So don't be shy. Ask lots of questions. Think of this as an education in your fashionable future happiness. These stores also likely stock various containers and other creative storage tools that will help simplify the organizational process and will make your day-to-day dressing faster and more efficient.

The Container Store, Target, and Bed Bath & Beyond are some of my favorite places to shop for containers and closet organizers. One piece of advice: Know what you need before you go. Make a list and go through it item by item to make sure there is a specific use for each thing. Also ensure that any of the items you need, especially containers or boxes, will actually fit in your closet. That is why it is so important to write down the specific measurements of your closet space. It's a good idea to prepare for your shopping trip to these giant and often overwhelming stores by taking a tour of their websites. You can check online to see what they offer in the store, which will keep you from bingeing once you enter the real bricks and mortar. These places can be like candy stores to children, filled with all kinds of gadgets and things you think you need until the sugar rush wears off and you realize this stuff is actually producing more piles of excess.

SPACE SAVERS

A double closet rod is a great space saver since it doubles your hanging space. The floor space under the lower rod is useful for storing a variety of clear containers, boxes, and cubbies that you can build yourself or purchase premade. Use these containers to store off-season clothing such as bathing suits, sweaters, and so on. Moving out of the closet for one brief moment, don't forget about the space under your bed. It's a great place to store off-season pieces and suitcases that you're not using for travel (these suitcases can also do double duty as off-season storage bins). You can purchase a variety of containers to store shoes by the pair under your bed. Just make sure these bins are relatively transparent so that you can get a clear view of each pair of shoes to cut your search time in half.

CLOSET ACCESSORIES

Go ahead and buy those extra shelves or organization racks for belts, scarves, and jewelry. If you don't want to shell out the money for these specialty items (and I applaud your frugality), the same organization of your accessories can be achieved with a variety of boxes, bins, separators, hooks, and nails. Be on the lookout for great organizer trays and dividers that can simplify your fashionable life. The more you divide, the easier it is to conquer! Don't forget to purchase thick plastic hangers that won't bend or break to replace all wire hangers, which ruin clothes. For suits, jackets, and coats, opt for sculpted hangers that hold the shape of the shoulder. The hangers in your closet should be uniform. This not only saves space, since various shapes won't be competing against each other, but the visual of uniform hangers is pleasing to the eye. The best stores in town don't use different hangers, so why should you? Don't forget mirrors to examine the new you and your newly redefined wardrobe. A full-length mirror can usually be placed on the front or back of your closet door.

THE HAMPER

It's a good idea to invest in a new hamper or two. You can split clothing that needs washing (separate your whites and darks).

Or, if you have a small closet, you can hang a couple of bags on hooks on the interior walls of the closet or on the inside of the closet door. It is also smart to add a bag for dry cleaning. Since I don't have enough room in my closet for my dry-cleaning storage, I found a beautiful decorative trunk that doubles as a table in my bedroom to put my dry cleaning in. Think outside the box when it comes to stashing your dirty laundry. Your job here is to do anything to maximize the property value that's inside of your closet and promote organization instead of chaos. Make sure all containers and shelves make sense organizationally and aesthetically. You don't want to have the cluttered look after you have spent all this time digging and sorting.

Clothing Organization

Now that you have your shelves, rods, containers, and hampers all smartly organized, it's time to put the goods back into the closet. This has to be done with the Blochbuster Grouping Method to give you easy access for crafting those amazing outfits. I break down my groupings of clothing by style, type, and color. All the shirts go into one group, then all the skirts, then the jackets, and so forth. The place I store each group in the closet mimics the way you dress. I begin from top to bottom as you would wear the clothes on your body. This means jackets and shirts on top, pants and skirts toward the bottom, and shoes on the floor. All of these clothing types will now be living together but separated into blacks, grays, navies, and so on. I work the system like a

WEATHER RELATED

Make sure your closet reflects the change of seasons if you live in a climate where the weather changes. You should store your clothing from last season in your attic or even under your bed in plastic containers to minimize possible damage from moths and moisture. Vacuum-sealer packs advertised on TV are also a good solution for storing off-season clothing. And don't forget: There's no need to throw out old suitcases. You can recycle them and use them to pack up seasonal clothing. Make sure when you buy suit-cases that they can fit under your bed so that you can get them out of the fray! Remember that when it comes to your closet, you only want to look at the clothes that you can wear right now. I don't want you to be staring at those heavy sweaters in the heat of summer, thinking that you don't have anything to wear.

color wheel. Group all of the blues together (from pastel to navy) in one section and do the same for the other colors. Group patterns and prints according to their main color and place them at the end of the respective color group. This is a fantastic system that will make it a cinch to find the exact pair of pink capris or the gray cropped blazer you need to cap off your look. It will also show you how much you own and in what colors.

Accessory and Shoe Organization

The last step will be to find little nooks of space to neatly house your jewelry and other accessories, which will be organized by type. All the necklaces and bracelets will be in their special place while winter accessories such as gloves and scarves will occupy a container with a divider down the middle. Group your undergarments together if you don't keep them in a chest of drawers. Make sure to organize your shoes

---

BLOCHBUSTER TIP

Become your own stylist! Does it always seem like you never have enough time in the morning to down a glass of juice let alone pick out a great outfit? Well then, set aside a rainy Saturday or Sunday and play stylist. Create a photo log of different outfits and ensembles. Pairing perfect separates is tough to figure out at 5 A.M. when you're still half asleep! A great idea I use with all my celebrity clients is to tape the photos onto a board on the inside of the closet door so that they have easy visual access to them. Or place them in a clothing photo album to hang from a string on a hook or the doorknob on the inside of the closet. It doesn't matter where, as long as it's easily visible for your early morning curtain call.

---

so that they're resting in pairs (one shoe facing forward and one facing backward to maximize space). In my own closet, I actually added extra shelves at the very bottom in order to store more shoes. Most shoes aren't more than six inches high, so with one foot of space on the ground of your closet, you can store two levels of shoes. I also suggest grouping your shoes into work shoes, dress shoes, and casual shoes. Again, it is helpful to divide by color and material so that you can see exactly what's there and what goes with what at a quick glance.

Food for Thought

You finally took action to get your finances in order through cleaning out your closet, taking a long, hard look at each and every item that has been living there for ages, and knowing what you own and what you have hoarded. In what ways do you think your chaotic closet affected your financial life?

_____

_____

_____

Has it ever crossed your mind that if you did clean your closet, perhaps you just might get a grip on your finances?

When and under what circumstances did you think in this way before reading this book?

_____

_____

_____

How did you feel when you made the commitment to go through with cleaning out your closet (be honest, please)?

_____

_____

What feelings did you experience during the first part of this process? Did these feelings change as the process continued? What did you feel when you sorted through the piles?

_____

_____

_____

Was this process empowering, or did you find it disabling or boring? How? Why?

_____

_____

_____

List five areas in which the process of cleaning your closet can and will benefit your budget. How does this feel?

1. _____

2. _____

3. _____

4. _____

5. _____

List at least two simple things you can do every day to keep this new frame of mind growing and thriving for the rest of your life. Do you think that simplifying will empower you?

1. _____

2. _____

꩜

This is major. You have this amazing closet, a mecca of organization and sanity. It's a reflection of the new you: clean, simple, and chic. That's something many people would pay a ton of money to have. (In fact, I know a lot of people in Hollywood who *have* paid a lot of money for that.) You deserve a reward—maybe a little shopping? You certainly have made space for a few new goodies. We are almost there. *Almost.* Before you hit the sales and stores again, we need to assess exactly what you are missing from your wardrobe in order to make it complete. Take a moment (and a deep breath) to sit in front of your closet and get Zen. Think about all the questions you just answered. You have gained full control of your past purchases. Use your clean new closet as inspiration as we move on to Step Eight, which is all about figuring out what you still need to look your best.

Satisfy Your Wardrobe Needs

You have now successfully weeded out the old, tired, and ugly from your wardrobe. Your closet has become your own personal store, as seductive and tempting as any boutique. And you are the proud owner and head buyer, carefully keeping tabs on the inventory necessary to satisfy the constantly changing needs of your best customer—you! Your new clean closet makes it so much easier to pinpoint exactly what's missing from your wardrobe. Now we will see just how to fill in those gaps.

People often ask me what is the must-have piece of clothing that should be in every closet. There's no one universal answer to this question: It depends on each person's body type, lifestyle, and personal style. But there are general rules that everyone should follow. Just as with food, we each have different nutritional needs that are dictated by our own unique bodies. Still, the FDA has set daily intake requirements that everyone should follow as guidelines for good nutrition. Well, just consider me your other FDA—your Fashion and Designer Authority! You already have the Clothing Pyramid. Now I will give you the specifics of what belongs in your closet. I will teach you how to add and subtract depending on your own taste and needs. We will also cover the essential do's and don'ts for work, a place where women spend a lot of hours but not with a lot of fashion inspiration. Then we will take a look at a few "closet cases"—real-life wardrobes that have multiple lessons to offer.

The most important thing to remember is that you don't need a lot of clothes. Yes, you might desire racks and drawers full of beautiful things, but it's not crucial. In fact, too much of a good thing (think ice cream *or* stilettos) can be harmful. Step Eight will show you that you can have great style with fewer items than you ever imagined.

What Every Great Closet Should Contain

I recommend the items in this section for their versatility, functionality, and simplicity. These essentials span many basic clothing needs. In the long run, having these transformational pieces will save you time and money because they will give your preexisting wardrobe a broader range of possibilities. But just because I'm suggesting that these are good items to own doesn't mean I want you to run out right now and bust your budget. Be wise and have patience. You don't lose all the weight you want to lose in a day, so you don't need to buy all of these recommended items in one, either. Take your time. Look for sales and deals. Stay focused. Use your self-restraint and good taste. Only buy under the right economic circumstances and at a time that is appropriate for you and your *Shopping Diet*. No more debt drama, please.

Once you've gone through my checklist of essentials, write down the pieces of clothing that are missing from your closet. Although the roster of wardrobe MVPs (Most Valuable Pieces) should guide you in making your list, you can refer to your clothing journal from Step Two and the star style category you chose in Step Three for a complete picture of what you need. Also keep in mind the body parts that you want to emphasize—this will help narrow down your purchases even further, say from a white shirt to a cap-sleeve white shirt. Make a detailed wish list in a notebook you keep in your closet and take with you on shopping trips.

LINGERIE

As every architect knows, before you build a building, you have to start with the proper foundation. And every stylist knows that before you put on any outfit, you have to start with the right foundations. Everyone is different, so in choosing the lingerie that you require, keep in mind the little extras that your specific body type may need to give you the perfect shape to showcase your clothes. The nude strapless convertible bra is a must, no matter your shape or size. Nude will go under every color and the convertible style will work with every neckline. Whether it has padding, underwire, minimal or complete coverage will depend on your body, your comfort level, and the desired effect you want to give. Another mandatory item is the white contoured T-shirt bra. This will give you a sleek and smooth silhouette under the tightest of tees or tanks. These bras are purposefully free of frills, lace, or bows that can look lumpy or bumpy under a fitted shirt.

As for the bottom half, this is really a matter of preference. Whether it's bikinis, briefs, boy shorts, full coverage, or the oh-so-daring thong—it's a matter of personal taste. However, comfort should play a factor in your decision. There's no need to suffer when there are cute undies in all styles. The fabric you intend to wear over your underwear is another factor when picking a pair of panties. For clinging jersey bottoms, I suggest a thong in an equally slinky fabric. No one wants to suffer from VPLs (Visible Panty Lines). Though all the girly trims and details may be sexy for the bedroom (unless you're Carrie Bradshaw or Madonna attempting to sport the underwear as outerwear trend . . . but realistically, most people's lifestyles can't afford that luxury, thank goodness!), your primary concern when it comes to essential lingerie is function and fit. And no one wants to see those ribbons and bows protruding from your posterior while wearing a slinky dress or low-cut pant. Again, nude is the preferred color. Many fabrics may not seem transparent in the dressing room, but by the light of day they could tell a different story. Nude tones will easily blend with most skin tones, making for a barely there look.

And for those whose food diet hasn't caught up to their *Shopping Diet,* shapewear is in style whether you're in Hollywood or your hometown. These high-performance shape shifters are not your grandmother's girdle. As mentioned earlier in the book, Hanes, Leggs, and Maidenform have created lines of affordable shape-shifting items. Maidenform's is called Flexees; they are perfect for fat-free dressing. Two of my favorite pieces in the collection are the camisoles and T-shirts, which act not only as tummy-tucking underwear but also as stylish and simple outerwear. They offer all the comfort and control you could ever want at a great price. It just goes to show you—the secret to looking fabulous isn't always about what's on the outside. Sometimes it really is about what's on the inside . . . and what's practical and affordable!

THE DRESS

If you can only afford one dress, make sure it's a dress that goes from day to evening. I suggest a simple sheath dress that fits perfectly in black or another dark neutral color like navy. This style can be worn on a variety of occasions. Think Audrey Hepburn—you can dress it up or you can dress it down with different accessories such as pins or belts or layers like blazers or cardigans.

If your budget is big enough for two dresses, then add a summer sundress in a vibrant color. This way, you have one dress that's more subdued and appropriate for evening and one that shines for daytime fun. The sundress should still be able to go from dawn to dusk if necessary. Find a style that can be worn under a jacket or sweater at the office but still appear romantic in the moonlight.

If you are planning on spending for a few more frocks, go for another dress that is all about being office appropriate yet still has a transformational quality to take it into an evening look. I love the flattering wrap dress. A scoop-neck dress is extremely versatile. In colder months, you can even layer it by putting a long-sleeve shirt or turtleneck underneath, or you can top it off by wearing it with a cardigan or blazer.

Now, if you really want to go dress crazy, another style that should be on your list is the shirtdress. You can have a lot of fun with the belt: Try a vibrant sash for an extra splash of color or a long necklace for an unusual twist. The shirtdress does double duty as a tunic for a more casual look, but you can always dress it up with heels for a night out. For the latter, make it a little sexier by unbuttoning some of those buttons. If you're going to break the dress bank (only if you have the actual funds in the bank, please!), then add one sexy party girl number that's either short and sparkly or with a fitted top and a fuller skirt.

THE SUIT

Everyone must have a black or navy suit in an all-weather wool blend that can work for multiple seasons. If you've got the funds, the next two colors of choice should be brown or gray. And if it suits your budget, go for a summertime splurge and pick up a tan, cream, or light gray suit in wrinkle-proof lightweight cotton. Last but no less luxurious, go for a linen suit or one in a bright color like red or cobalt blue.

Style-wise, I would recommend a matching pant and jacket suit with an accompanying skirt that also matches or comes in a complementary color, plaid, or pinstripe. Let's say you have the classic black pantsuit with the black jacket that works for the big CEO meeting. The next day, create a whole different outfit by combining the jacket, another shirt, and the complementary skirt. This variety will give you more dash for your cash. It creates a multitude of looks that are not so "matchy" and gives you a hint of personal style. Today's woman wants her own individual look, and that skirt with the bold stripe or plaid may do the trick.

If you want to get funky and buy three pieces, then make it a pantsuit with a matching or contrasting vest. Masculine tailored looks have been in fashion since the days of Marlene Dietrich. Leave the jacket at home and wear the vest alone with the pants for an updated twist on an office classic. It's sexy secretary with a little Annie Hall twist. To propel the look even more fashion forward, throw on a fedora or newsboy cap.

When buying a suit, stay away from the extremes in lapels and pant legs. Stick to the straight silhouette and avoid trends like high waists and bell bottoms. Jacket lengths also tend to rise and fall with the seasons. But as we've learned in previous chapters, the most popular look of the season might not be what's best for you. It can also become dated very easily. Always keep your body type and signature style in mind when picking out a suit. When buying the extra pieces to accompany, complement, and enhance the suit, go for something a little more trend conscious such as a vibrant silk blouse, a wide-leg pant, a full skirt, a bold gold necklace, or a graphic print scarf. These items, which should be less of a financial investment than your suit, can have a shorter shelf life.

THE CHANEL-INSPIRED JACKET

You don't have to run out and buy Chanel to get that iconic look. I'm talking about the classic style, which is the perfect deconstructed jacket with a round collar that's easy to accessorize with chain necklaces, beads, pearls, brooches, and scarves. Play with proportions by layering different collar styles underneath the jacket. It's versatile in that you can dress it up or down depending on what you choose to pair it with from your closet boutique. You can match it with some of the previous suiting pieces for an elegant look. Or create contrast with a tank, tee, or turtleneck. You can even pair it with your favorite jeans for a super-chic ensemble. The simplicity of the jacket's silhouette and design makes it entirely multipurpose. I love that this is a feminine alternative to the classic men's-cut blazer. Buy it in a rich textured fabric such as bouclé or tweed.

THE CARDIGAN

A cardigan is a great way to stay warm and fashionable all at once. You can wear this sweater to work or as a great neutral item on the weekend. In the office, match your cardigan with your suiting separates. For a night on the town, layer it over your flirty dress to protect you from getting chilly. It's also a great cover-up for the sleeveless tops for those who don't wish to show their arms. The crew-neck style is always a classic, but a shawl or V-neck collar is a fun and modern alternative. Whatever the style, make sure the sweater is good quality and a good fit. You should be able to button it up completely without straining the fabric. The cardigan is the perfect place to throw a splash of pop color into your wardrobe, so break the boundaries of basic black with pastels and rich jewel tones.

THE WHITE-COLLAR SHIRT

The white-collar shirt runs the risk of being a tad cliché. An obvious staple, it can easily be boring and unimaginative. To make your white shirt extraordinary, go for something with pin tucks, pleating, or ruffles. Let the white-collar shirt be an event—a clean, crisp conversation piece. It's easy to find one with beautiful buttons or a dramatic collar or sleeve. Or find one with a chic masculine touch that's adorned with cuff links. These types of details will take your white shirt from staid to standout.

THE FIVE TOPS

Here are the five tops that every woman needs in her wardrobe: V-neck, boatneck, turtleneck, scoop neck, and classic. The ideal is to have these five tops in a variety of colors and fabrics, as that is what draws attention to your face. Remember, you can save by buying in bulk, especially if there is a sale. An in-store brand is also a perfect way to stock up and save money on classic styles. Find the variation on each of these styles that suits you. For example, a modern update of the classic shirt would be something with a ruffle or bows, but don't let those details overpower you. If you find a scoop neck too revealing and a boatneck doesn't enhance your neck, try a sweetheart neckline, a crew neck, or even a wrap top.

The important thing is to have shirts with different necklines to create various looks.

Make sure your five tops come in different colors, ranging from classic solids in neutral tones and pastels to shout-out colors or even prints. I would include at least one shirt in white, black, gray, or brown because those shades complement most anything you can think of. If you are only going to have a few tops, then keep patterns to a minimum. Patterns stay with the memory longer, so it's best to save them to wear once a month. Otherwise, your coworkers will think you wear the same top every day!

Consider different sleeve lengths on your shirts as well. Three-quarter-length sleeves or bracelet sleeves are the new classics to keep in mind. One practical note: You can always make a long-sleeve top into a short-sleeve one by rolling up those sleeves, but a cap sleeve will never keep you warm on a cold day.

JEANS

If you only have one pair of jeans, skip the embellishments and faded lines and go for a simple dark wash in the most flattering cut and width for your legs and butt. A modern and unadorned pair of jeans is a life, and style, saver. These jeans, which can be worn 24/7, can be made casual or dressy depending on your choice of accessories. If you can get two pairs of jeans, then opt for a straight-leg pair and a wide-leg pair (but only if both work for your silhouette). Avoid the extremes when it comes to the waistline. Jeans that are high in the waist are too trendy. As for those low, low, low-ride jeans, please just say no to crack.

THE PURSE

If you want to be economical, then opt for a bag in traditional black or brown leather. These classics will carry you far. Suede is nice, but it attracts dust and dirt, especially if you use it as your staple bag. If you can spend a little more, also buy a flirty beaded evening clutch in a dark tone to glam up a basic outfit at night. Don't start sweating at the thought of shelling out $5,000 for that Fendi Baguette. Vintage stores are a great place to find a good deal on these little numbers. With all the money you save thrifting, you can buy an oversized tote that doubles as a weekend bag for any fabulous jaunts you have planned. The bigger-size bags do give the appearance of smaller hips as well—it's all about proportions!

BROWN OR BLACK PUMPS

Just like the staple bag, every woman needs a pair of black or brown pumps. This style and color will go with so many outfits that the only additional money you'll have to spend will be on repairing the soles from so much wear. For even more versatility, you can use clip-on earrings as an adornment that switches this daytime shoe into a nighttime knockout. If your shoe budget permits another key purchase (and it should, because no woman should be asked to step out in style with just one footwear option), then consider a pair in patent leather or metallic. If a stiletto is too much for your work world, try a wider heel, a platform heel, a kitten heel, or a wedge for a comfortable yet classy addition to your shoe closet.

When you're ready for your next splurge, you should buy a pair of flesh-tone heels that will make your legs look longer. An alternative to the nude shoe is a faux snakeskin with caramel cream and black tones. These shoes will go with everything from browns to blacks to creams and will take you from your desk to the dance floor.

Next on the list is a pair of strappy summer shoes with a bit of height. If heels aren't your thing, then give a pair of flats or a wedge a whirl. I'm sure you'll find some way to fulfill your shoe fetish and achieve a well-balanced heel.

COATS

You definitely need one functional and versatile coat in navy, camel, black, or gray. The cut, length, and silhouette must be flattering to fit your body type. You never want an overcoat to be overbearing. Don't forget: A coat should keep you warm! That's the point, right? Wool or wool/cashmere blends are the best for staying toasty. There's nothing worse than choosing style over function in a winter coat.

Another great tip is to take your coat to the dry cleaner and have it waterproofed. It's a small investment that you will thank me for on the next rainy day. I often do it myself with a store-bought can of waterproof spray, which saves even more. If you can afford a second coat, then go for a great trench—it is timeless when purchased in a classic color. This fuller silhouette with a belt to cinch the waist flatters all figures by camouflaging the hips and complements all clothing styles. It works in all kinds of weather and is perfect for layering. When coat shopping, make sure that the lining is durable and warm. Many times, you can find a coat that features a detachable lining and can be worn through all seasons.

WORK WEAR

Unless you work in a very corporate environment where it's all dark suits all the time, figuring out what to wear at the office can be a frustrating fashion experience. Like you need any more pressure from your job! You want to look cute and cool but also appropriate. That's a tricky negotiation that I have to help my clients with all the time. Here are my rules for looking pretty *and* professional.

In the last few seasons, designers have created a plethora of wearable and multifunctional jersey dresses that would love to have a place in your closet. Dresses in a soft jersey are perfect for the office because they're easy to move around in and are adverse to wrinkles. They are easily paired with anything from a cardigan to a jacket. Hand washable, the material is perfect for taking on business trips. (You can wash them in the evening, hang them up to dry on the shower rod, and they're ready and waiting to go in the morning when you are.) Dress them up or down with stockings or tights and match with boots or pumps depending on the season or your mood. This is a practical way to get through the workday without feeling like you're in a uniform.

Another solution to office dressing is the twinset. I'm not talking about your grandmother's twinset. You don't need to buy your twins as a set, but find complementary pieces that work well together. Buy a shell or a T-shirt and pair it with a cardigan. I do suggest that you buy those pieces on the same day so that you will have them in your hot little hands and know that they play well together. This look can easily be transported into the weekend or casual time: Throw these multipurpose sweater separates over a dress, skirt, or even wear them with jeans. You can also layer a camisole under your cardigan and wear it that way to the office. Just make sure that this look is not too lingerie-ish and that you aren't showing the other twins. That's not professional unless you work at Hooters.

BLOCH**BUSTER TIP**

You know how hard it is to get up in the morning, open your closet, and fumble around for something smart to wear. Try this old-school tip courtesy of your mom! Get your outfit for work ready the night before. Hang the outfit on a special hook on the back of your closet door. For many of my celebrity clients, we often set up several days' and nights' worth of outfit options in advance. Space permitting, I recommend placing these go-to looks on a separate rack or in a separate section in your closet. Personally, I use a rolling rack that I keep in my bedroom so that these outfits are visible and easily accessible to me at all times. If I have leisure time around the house on the weekends, I take a moment to set up the outfits I plan on wearing in the week to come. Do the same for any upcoming special events you might have. Your bonus will be that you can sleep in a little longer.

NEVER AT THE OFFICE

The one dress that's never appropriate for the office is that peasant number that flows to the floor and makes it seem like you're ready to return to Woodstock. Theme looks, like cowboy boots and jeans, also don't work for work. The roaring '20s flapper style is great for a cocktail party but should be put on prohibition when you're in your cubicle.

Miniskirts are an acquired taste—make sure you've acquired enough taste to know how to wear them. Anything tight or shorter than a few inches above the knee, and you're treading in dangerous territory. Most important, your legs have to make the miniskirt cut. Don't wear them at all unless you have great gams.

A white or colored T-shirt can work at the office, but avoid logo tees at all costs . . . unless you work at Costco. You can even wear a casual tank top or tee when covered with a jacket or a cardigan and complemented by statement jewelry. It's okay to add a little sparkle for a daytime meeting but not too much. Remember, a little sparkle goes a long way. Skintight or leather pants are a no-no. The same is true for shorts, even in the summer.

Closet Cases ⌒

There are as many ways to organize your closet and fill out your wardrobe as there are clothes in the mall. That's why finding the solution to whatever dilemmas you face in your own closet can be overwhelming. I have had the honor of helping many women clean their closets so that they can shed the confusion that usually greets them before they get dressed. Using the principles discussed so far in *The Shopping Diet,* we found practical solutions to their real-life problems. In the process, I have learned a lot about how my guidelines take different forms depending on who is using them. Let's peek inside the closets of a few of my fabulous and fashionable friends.

CASE STUDY: Heidi and Darren

As newlyweds, Heidi and Darren were adjusting to their new lives together in Heidi's small Manhattan condominium. Heidi, an accomplished businesswoman and owner of Krupp Group, a public relations firm, leads a whirlwind life of meetings, lunches, dinners, book tours, and red-carpet events. Her clothing needs are varied and must include both business wear for work and casual wear for the weekends in the city or traveling with her handsome husband. She also needs formal wear for those special occasions.

This couple loves to shop. (They consider a sample sale the most wonderful way to spend a Saturday together.) These two typical New Yorkers have a department store's worth of clothes and not a lot of closet space to spare. As a result, their small closets had become scary places. Heidi has a big personality and loves flamboyant items. But she needed to learn how to edit her closet down before the contents took over her (and her husband's) new life.

SHOPPING SYMPTOMS

"The truth is, I can never find anything I want to wear," Heidi confessed to me. It's no wonder. When I opened her bursting-at-the-hinges closet, I found it was suffering from an orange O.D. The woman literally has more orange than Hermès. Just because you like a color, doesn't mean you have to drown in it. This is why I suggest color grouping your clothes to see how much you really have in one color. In Heidi's case, there were about twenty-five orange pieces including sweaters, sweatshirts, T-shirts, tank tops, crew necks, thermals, and even an orange cashmere zip-up jacket.

The problem with Heidi's orange fixation wasn't just that all the clothing was the same color. Most also fell into the casual clothes group (a.k.a. the veggies section of our Clothing Pyramid). If the color had been dispersed across dresses, coats, and blazers, I might have allowed her to keep more of her signature hue. But the truth was that her orange collection was basically the same piece repeated over and over again. These citrus-saturated pieces were all in the same relative style and made from the same mid-weight material.

I used to joke with Heidi that she had "camisoles disease." During her single girl days, every time that she left the house, she felt that she had to buy something to make herself feel better. Weight has been an up-and-down issue for her throughout the years, so camisoles were an easy fit. The addiction was not necessarily to camisoles but to spending. The result was about thirty camisoles in her closet. Her camisoles do add a great feminine touch under a masculine tailored suit. For example, her leopard camisole is perfect under a black suit for the office. Then she can shed the jacket for an evening out. But she certainly didn't need so many!

KEEPERS

Amid Heidi's bright orange wardrobe, we focused on a cashmere scoop-neck sweater with white piping. This ended up being a great piece because she could dress it up or down. She was also only allowed to keep the orange zip-up. Everything else juicy went into the donation pile.

One of the first things I instantly threw into the keepers pile was her little black Prada dress. The piece was in perfect condition. The hemline was midknee classic, and it's a dress that she will get years of use out of. This was a no-brainer, and, of course, I had bought it for her!

FIXERS

Heidi looked a bit sad when she handed me her favorite print silk blouse that used to have the most romantic poet sleeves with elastic in the wrists to keep them puffy. The material was still gorgeous, but the elastic was worn and now those same sleeves hung like they were dead flowers. She had refused to toss it, and lucky for her, I had the fix. We sent the shirt to the tailor to sew a black velvet ribbon where the elastic once was and then tie a bow at the end.

Heidi handed me a $795 Dolce & Gabbana jacket that she had found at a sample sale for $100, which made it a great buy—except that the jacket was too big. That nice sample sale surprise had sat in her closet for so long, it could have gone out of style. But it hadn't, and the material was incredible. Because it's easier to take in a big jacket than let out a smaller one, Heidi was able to make this work with a few nips and tucks at the tailor.

Darren is a fashion savant and found a great present for his new wife. "He took all of my shoes to the shoemaker and reheeled them," Heidi marveled. (I love this man!) Yes, it cost $40 a pair, but it was a great way to save $500 Manolos from the trash bin. "Heidi is tough on shoes," Darren explained. "The shoemaker balanced the shoes and even reinforced the heels. He resurfaced some of the leather and glazed some of the shoes." In the end, Heidi didn't buy any new shoes that season, thanks to her new husband's thoughtful gift. It's another lesson on how maintaining your clothes will save you money . . . and maybe your marriage!

GIVEAWAYS

The clothes that didn't fit into any group that I'd ever heard of—like her Wild West dress in Southwestern colors—immediately hit the giveaway pile.

Her big revelation was about a large paisley dress/poncho from a Gucci sample sale. She told me that she had bought it when she was heavier, but Heidi was now working out, eating right, and looking great. She had a nice waist, but still she clutched that Gucci poncho to her chest and cried, "I don't want to throw it out because it's Gucci!" I looked her dead in the eyes and asked her what part of her body she thought it enhanced. It made her look shorter and heavier—two words nobody wants to hear about their look. "And you've worked so hard at the gym to have a shape," I argued. I asked her to try it on and take a hard look. In the end, the poncho that fit like a camping tarp was tossed into the consignment pile. A designer label shouldn't make it a keeper if it doesn't make your body look better.

CLOSET ORGANIZATION

One of our first steps was to take all of the casual clothes out and toss them on the bed for careful evaluation. It didn't take long until we had the casual clothing into several piles that reflected Heidi's casual life needs: gym clothes, weekend clothes, and nicer casual clothing for a day of shopping or a night at the movies. Now that Heidi knows what she has, and how much of it, it's easy to refrain from buying more of the same.

She had also committed the unpardonable sin of keeping her expensive cashmere sweaters on wire hangers from the cleaners with the plastic bags still on them. Not to sound like the Joan Crawford of fashion here, but let me say one more time, *No more wire hangers!* If you continue to use bad hangers, then the material will stretch and eventually ruin the original shape of the sweater. If you have cashmere, wool, or fine knits, take them off those clothes-killing hangers immediately. Fold them and place them in a drawer or on a shelf. Don't forget the cedar chips to keep the moths away. Cashmere costs way too much to be a moth's midnight snack. If you must hang your sweaters, use velvet or silk hangers designed specifically for storing finer pieces. They will be less likely to leave hanger marks on the item. Return those wire hangers from whence they came: the dry cleaner, to be recycled!

Because Heidi has so much good clothing, I suggested that she pick out a few jackets she didn't think she would wear that year and—as they say in Hollywood—put them on hiatus. Either put them in storage to allow more room in a cramped city apartment or lend them to a friend for a season. It's a great way to help someone get a new look without spending any money. Just make sure you lend the clothing to a friend who will keep it in good condition and pick a date to return it.

EXTRA CREDIT

It must be noted that Heidi has the perfect shoe closet, which means there is a bit of everything with no redundancy. The shoes were not in some sort of nightmare jumble but organized (by color and style) in a metal shoe organizer that hangs from the inside of her closet door. She has heels, flats, and boots in the basic colors of black, gray, and brown in both designer labels and some funkier finds, including studded boots from Hong Kong and animal-print party heels. There are a couple of nude-colored shoes that make the leg look longer and statement heels with crystal embellishments such as big diamond buckles. Heidi knows what she likes and has pointy toe and higher-heeled shoes that aren't stilettos. This is the key to a great shoe closet—variety and usability.

CASE STUDY: Belinda

Belinda is a chic and tall business consultant and movie producer. An eclectic type who lives in Harlem, she loves to pour over fashion magazines and is up on the latest trends, even if she doesn't always feel the need to buy or buy into them. She used to make her own clothing when she had more time, so she knows how to spot high quality. In fact, she will scrutinize an item's construction and material before she decides to make a purchase.

It's clear that Belinda is a savvy shopper who knows how to mix cheaper pieces with designer classics. It was my job to point this talent out to her and also discreetly inform her that some of her pieces just did not work together. She had problems with deciding what to keep and what to toss, so I needed to walk her through the process of how to make those final choices that would trim the excess and punch up her signature style.

SHOPPING SYMPTOMS

Belinda is by no means a huge shopper—in fact, her closet was a bit anorexic. "I'm all about the basics and the key pieces," she said. "Plus, I don't want to be in debt, so I don't go overboard on clothes." Yet Belinda still had clothes in her two closets that needed to take a hike back to the 1980s.

KEEPERS

Most of Belinda's suits were in great condition and only a few years old, but she felt they were too formal for her current workplace. I suggested she wear them as separates to reinvigorate and reintegrate them back into her wardrobe. A great pair of suit pants paired with a sweater gave her a totally new and chic outfit.

For evening, we kept her sexy 1930s-inspired cocktail dress and a flattering halter dress in pink, since both items still looked great on her without revealing too much flesh.

I'm not usually one to talk people into keeping clothes, but there was a black skirt covered in embroidered flowers that Belinda wanted to give away because she thought the style was too bohemian. I showed her an alternative way to wear it—with a solid top and flat shoe. Suddenly, it had an ethnic-inspired look and became a fun summer outfit. Belinda put the skirt back in her closet.

FIXERS

Belinda had a bag full of stuff that needed adjusting. For Christmas last year, she asked her boyfriend for a sewing machine, determined to fix the pieces herself in order to save money. (She is definitely ahead of *The Shopping Diet* learning curve in many ways!) However, it helps to realize what can and cannot be fixed. Belinda can certainly fix the seams of a jacket that are pulling apart. And she can definitely cut down those pants that were yards too long. But taking them in at the thigh would be a little too challenging. I forced her to either spend money on a tailor or banish them to the donation pile.

Two items that weren't in the pile but we decided to make alterations to were a velvet robe and an old bridesmaid's dress. We decided to shorten the designer black velvet robe to make it into the perfect evening coat, switching out the bathrobe belt for a silk tasseled one to create a sophisticated look. The pale pink bridesmaid's dress was easily cut down to a sexy top to be paired with skinny jeans for a night on the town.

GIVEAWAYS

Belinda is a dress girl, yet immediately we hauled out a wrap dress that hit her too high in the torso and made her uncomfortable. There is no use harboring clothing that you will never wear. We also nixed a little plaid miniskirt and sent it to the consignment shop because Belinda and I both felt it was no longer age appropriate.

An Escada suit from London circa 1991 was a tougher decision. Ultimately, its very close fitted jacket and too-short skirt sadly sent this one to the consignment store. It truly was not wearable for Belinda, who admitted to feeling uncomfortable flashing that much leg these days.

Belinda's tight Tina Turner black dress was tossed into the giveaway bag as was a masculine-looking leather jacket that she just "couldn't rock anymore." The overembellished designer suit jacket that originally had a big price tag and screamed *Dynasty* was a perfect item to sell on eBay.

Her charity bag kept expanding as we added an older black sweater that was too pilled to repair, a red quilted blazer that Ralph Lauren wouldn't have sent on the hunt, and a boxy suit that would have even made fashionistas from the '80s balk.

GETS

Even though we're trying to save money in *The Shopping Diet,* there were certain pieces that I felt were lacking in Belinda's closet. One MIA staple was the perfect pair of black or brown suit pants. (I suggested she try Tanger Outlets, Loehmann's, or Kohl's, where she would easily be able to afford them.) These are easy pieces to find, and she could combine them with a simple shirt and blazer (that she already owns) for work.

Belinda is no Imelda Marcos. Her shoe selection was a bit

bland. She definitely needed to ease on down the road to DSW or Payless. She had classic black and brown pumps and a pair of sparkling green statement shoes that went well with her one and only formal gown. She also had a pair of functional black boots, lots of flats (Belinda's height conscious!), and a couple of pairs of sneakers, because she loves to run. I thought she should add some wedge platform sandals for the warmer weather—but nothing too high. She could even try a kitten heel for a dressier look that would still play down her height.

CLOSET ORGANIZATION

Belinda made an investment in an organized future by purchasing a multishelf Ikea modular wall unit with hanging racks. Because she can adjust the racks and shelves to fit her specific needs, Belinda can switch them in and out as she goes through different clothing phases.

Despite her efforts, she had committed a cardinal closet sin. Her fancy dresses were in plastic dry-cleaning bags just waiting for their next night on the town. But savvy closet makeover artists will rip that plastic off immediately. Storing clothing in plastic makes it sweat and ruins the fabric. If you had stains removed from an item, keeping it in plastic will often bring those stains right back to life, defeating the purpose of dry cleaning them in the first place.

Like most budget-conscious shoppers, Belinda is an accessories girl. Because of her height, she knows that belts are the perfect way to break up her torso. She did a great job of organizing her belts, first by color, then dividing and lining them up by width, from thickest to thin. She also had plastic containers packed with a jumble of cheaper jewelry. This was a problem area because she had no idea what she owned or how to even find it. I suggested taking a rainy Saturday afternoon to spread all her baubles out on her bed and organize them much the way she did her clothes: by type, such as necklaces or rings, and then by color or style.

EXTRA CREDIT

Belinda is very accepting of the idea that sizes vary, which is reflected in her closet, where she owns clothes in sizes from 6 to 12. Many women want to ditch clothing that was purchased in larger sizes. This is not a good idea. A size 12 from Zara might work for you, while your Calvin Klein dress reads size 6. In many cases, size doesn't matter. It's all about the fit, so don't discriminate based on what the tag says. Go for what fits you.

CASE STUDY: Pamela

Pamela is a forty-six-year-old mother of two adorable children, ages five and six. Before her kids were born, she was an assistant to a top movie studio executive and then an Academy Award–winning director. In this previous life, she was always on the go. But all that changed when she married and became a harried working mom. At 5'4", Pamela frets that she still hasn't been able to drop those twenty extra pounds after having her children. "I lose ten pounds, but they always end up finding me again," Pamela said. Her bra size has also increased quite a bit since giving birth, making most of her pre-maternal wardrobe obsolete.

You don't need to be a shopaholic to have fashion dilemmas. Pamela lived in four cities in just four years while her husband was establishing a new business. Between the moves, the children, the man, and the new life, there wasn't much time or money to spend on clothes. "On the weekends, if I have a free minute, I'd rather read a book than look for jeans," Pamela said. "I don't even own a pair of jeans or sweatpants and I really need help. I am all mixed up in the clothing area of my life."

In fact, Pamela didn't take me to her closet. She didn't need to. She brought out the ten well-edited items of clothing that she owns and wears nonstop in a little bag. "Before I got pregnant, I was a size 6 and I had beautiful clothes," she said. "But I've given those clothes away because they don't fit anymore. Plus, they're now too young for me. I can't wear miniskirts anymore. I want a more sophisticated look as a wife and a mother now. But unfortunately, I just don't know how or where to find what's missing from my wardrobe."

SHOPPING SYMPTOMS

It's obvious that Pamela has an underfed and malnourished closet. She wore a lovely gray sweater over a black turtleneck and black pleated pants. She pulled out a few extra clothing items that she wasn't wearing that day from her itty-bitty bag. She brought out two multicolored wool winter skirts, two multicolored flowing summer skirts, a pair of black slacks, a pair of navy pinstripe slacks, a black blazer that matched the pants that she was wearing, a brown DKNY suit jacket, and another summer skirt in cotton that she wears around the house. "That casual summer skirt has been worn to death," she confessed. "In the summer, I take the kids to the community pool and I wear it over my swimsuit."

Pamela's wardrobe also consisted of black, gray, and navy turtlenecks and a classic beige cardigan. She had one chocolate knitted sweater plus three lightweight summer blouses in white, lime green, and black.

It's not that Pamela enjoys minimalist dressing. Her family's finances and her lack of free time dictate her shopping parameters. I do give her major points for choosing all of those skirts in quality material and interesting patterns. They are classics that manage to reflect her personal style without being so distinct as to become a case of "there she is in that getup again."

GETS

"I just don't have the money to spend on a lot of clothes. I am sure I need them. Yet I am not sure what to get," Pamela said. She wanted whatever new purchases she made to be durable and of high quality. "After all, they have to last," she said.

What Pamela lacks and needs ASAP is sporty clothing to wear on the weekends and at night during family time with her husband and children. She doesn't even own a good pair of jeans! She's resisted buying denim, afraid that her curvaceous booty will force her into "mom jeans." "I don't have time to spend a day trying on a million pairs of jeans," she explained. I told her to do what moms do best—multitask! I asked her to study women on the train, on the streets, or at the office with similar bodies to hers to find those wearing jeans she likes. When she finds these women, she should ask what brand they are wearing. It's a time-efficient way to discover what will look great on you. In fact, you'll cut your shopping time in half. The next step for Pamela was to try on those jeans in various sizes and buy two pairs in dark blue denim. Presto, her jean needs were filled for the next few years.

In addition, I suggested Pamela invest in two more skirts—a black pencil skirt and a skirt with a trumpet bottom, because both are versatile, classic, and perfect for her body type. Anyone can look upscale on a low-scale budget by keeping it chic, simple, and well fitted. If you can only purchase a few pieces, stick to basic colors such as blacks, navies, browns, and olives, or other subtle tones. Tweed is a smart option if you are looking for a pattern, because people won't notice it as much as bold prints, which shout even if you wear them once a week.

Comfort is big in Pamela's world, so I advised her to look for clothes made with stretchier fabrics, such as a jersey dress, to accommodate her curves. She doesn't need her 5 A.M. wake-up time to be followed by a struggle with a pair of pants that aren't cooperating. She also desperately needed a hoodie and a pair of chic velvet or fancier sweatpants for weekend outings. A nice casual pair of black or navy pants would have also fit the bill.

EXTRA CREDIT

If you really don't have the time to shop, you can get an idea of what you want just by keeping your eyes on the prize. Just like Pamela did, observe what others are wearing well. Ask your friends or coworkers questions and let them help you do your fashion research in terms of stores and styles. Instead of roaming around aimlessly, you'll be able to hit the stores that cater to your exact needs. Give yourself a two-hour window to shop before you take a break or do something else. Internet and catalog shopping can be an effective alternative. I had Pamela use the time during a lunch break and after dropping the kids at school for a little style surfing. You can even do a little retail therapy after you've put them to bed for the evening. When you do find an item that looks great, buy in bulk. Who knows when you'll have the time to locate such a find again? So if that top works for you in cream, snag it in black and gray or a pop color for a splash of fun and a dash of style!

CASE STUDY: Alex

Alex, a gorgeous redhead in her twenties, is a professional in the fashion world and the first person I have met with a well-balanced closet. She moved from Canada to New York to study and now works as a personal assistant to . . . yours truly. Always stylish and on the cutting edge, Alex lives in a rented apartment that she shares with a roommate. "Living in New York City is rough," Alex said. "The joke is that no one who is young in the fashion business has any money to actually buy fashion!" But Alex always makes the best of what she has.

She knows how to take an inexpensive piece and turn it into something she loves—an ensemble that exudes glamour. She lives on the fashion websites to find out about all of the sample sales and makes sure she gets to them early, and only if she has the extra cash to burn. "I've had a few dreams come true at sample sales," Alex said. "It's a lot more civilized than people think and a hell of a lot more civilized than dating! No one gets hurt." No one, except her fashion findings that were jammed in a closet.

SHOPPING SYMPTOMS

Alex has a great combination of the fast fashion staples—such as inexpensive little black dresses, pop-colored pieces, and patterned cardigans—mixed in with several special designer pieces including blazers and tops. She likes very simple clothes or ones that have a unique twist to them that sets them apart and makes them stand out. She loves oversized layers of tailored pieces for an ironic and sartorial play on menswear, pairing an oversized white tuxedo shirt with a fitted vest, leggings, and a fedora. She also does a lot of vintage store shopping to find one-of-a-kind pieces. "You know that no one else will be wearing it, which is never guaranteed with those H&M disposable fashion finds," Alex said.

Alex is a classic buyer who has a lot of white, gray, and black. She has a few items in bright saturated colors like cobalt blue and purple. As a redhead, she says that very few patterns work for her. That's why she keeps graphics to a minimum and uses them to add a little excitement to her basic color scheme. She does go for ruffles or even poofy dresses, but downplays them by wearing them under a blazer or jacket. "I'm not afraid of sequins," she said. "But I'll just let them peek out from under another layer, like a cardigan or a coat." She takes a statement slinky piece and then plays down the sexy factor. Her lace tank is hidden under that oversized blazer.

THE KEEPERS

Alex already had the basics in my closet essentials list. I love that Alex knows her body—not wearing too many skirts because she feels her legs are too pale. In fact, she usually only wears short skirts with leggings or tights. (A tinted moisturizing cream could also solve that problem quickly.) I love that all of her shirts can be worn year-round. She has only a few short-sleeve tops, preferring to convert long-sleeve ones into short instead of being stuck with no sleeves at all. She certainly has enough sweaters and jeans, plus she owns a black pencil skirt and black trousers. I approved of all of it. Why not? It's in my book!

CLOSET ORGANIZATION

Her closet is color coded, but the various types of pieces are all over the place. So what she has is an eclectic mishmash of items all jammed together. Blazers live next to pants that dwell on top of cashmere sweaters. I love that the colors are together, but the styles should be separated as well. Her jeans are actually folded in a dresser drawer because she feels that they take up too much room in her closet. Alex may be a savvy shopper, but she's not using her storage and closet space to their potential. As a result, she has a tendency to forget the fabulous items she already owns, since they are not visible or easy to find.

Her expensive shoes—a nice variety of designer shoes and statement pieces like her neon pink satin pumps—were in soft shoe bags, yet the bags had no labels or photos of the shoes inside. We added the labels for the perfect organizational touch to make finding a particular pair easier.

Finding a ring or bracelet among Alex's mountains of accessories was a whole other story. She's the first one to admit that accessories are her major life splurge (besides her rent!). "Those are the things that separate me from the pack," Alex said. "You can wear the simplest of outfits, but pair it with a bold oversized necklace or a pop-color pump, and you'll get noticed. I collect a ton of jewelry." Her jewelry includes big statement pieces that she finds for sale on the street or at flea markets. She favors costume jewelry and has an extensive collection of vintage rhinestone bracelets and elaborate necklaces whose sparkle would blind even the most seasoned of Las Vegas showgirls. There were giant pearls hanging from her bedroom mirror and countless trays of jewelry inside her dresser drawers. Her large chains and pearls are perfect over a turtleneck, black sweater, or other simple silhouettes but not hung on her furniture. She has so many fabulous pieces—she deserves to be able to get to them easily and efficiently.

What Alex needed were storage solutions. Instead of hanging all her necklaces in clumps on the corner of a mirror, we used a series of hooks screwed into a wall or the door of a closet in order to keep them neat and untangled. I also love using acrylic trays with dividers for earrings, bracelets, and other bobbles—you can see everything at once, but everything is in its own compartment. If you are like Alex and have gone to the trouble of collecting these vintage signature jewelry pieces, treat them with respect. If you do, you'll be able to pass them down the family line to the next generation. I often suggest that Alex slow her roll, stay in her lane, and curb her enthusiasm on that vintage jewelry (especially since I know her salary!), but I know she won't listen to me because it's her passion. She's stubborn when it comes to what she loves . . . just like her boss. And that's why I love her!

We've done plenty of poking and prodding in some dark closets. Now I say, let there be light . . . and shopping! After comparing your real-life clothes to my ideal list, I can imagine that you've found multiple holes in your wardrobe that you're dying to plug. There's only one solution for that, and it's to hit the stores. But don't forget, you're still on *The Shopping Diet.* No more running into the biggest store in the closest mall to grab the most colorful item. Your new approach to shopping will be smart and streamlined—just like your closet waiting for you at home.

part three

The Ultimate Indulgence:
Your Super Self

Step Nine:

Practice Safe, Responsible Shopping

Insiders don't shop in a haphazard fashion. They don't walk into a store because the window display is screaming *sale!* They don't charge a dress just because a salesperson says it's the hottest style. They shop with a businesslike purpose that's filled with knowledge, skepticism, and restraint. Now is the time for you to employ the same approach. You are off to the right start. You have the space in your closet for a few additions; you know what you like; but more important, you know what you need.

In Step Nine, you'll learn the right places to shop in order to avoid the empty shopping calories of overpriced items, marketing gimmicks, and second-rate styles. Once you understand what each type of store has to offer, how to assess the quality of an item, and the way to make the most out of sales (plus, the best secrets for clothing, shoe, and bag shopping), you will make healthy, responsible choices because you are in control.

The Shopping Diet Log: Figuring Out Your Finances

Before we hit the stores, there are a couple of preliminary steps you definitely need to know in order to remain true to your budget. A good diet has you write down everything you eat because that's the only way to be accountable. Writing it down makes it official and also forces you to train yourself to recognize and even dread writing down something bad, so you just won't do it. It works this way with spending as well. Writing down what you have spent your money on is the only way to fess up to your spending problems and truly know what's going down in your life . . . and down the drain. You might not remember that taxi ride home from work because you couldn't bare the subway in those too-tight pumps or that makeup you threw into your cart while wheeling around the drugstore. But these added costs are hard to ignore when they're staring back at you in black and white. You must know how much you have been spending and what you can realistically spend on clothes.

What I want you to do is write down everything you spend. In order to see how many extra bucks you have in your *Shopping Diet,* you need to see how much you're buying versus how much you are earning on a monthly basis. It's time to face fiscal reality. The only way to do this is to take a long and very complete look at your finances. Many of us walk around in a financial fog, writing checks as needed, pulling cash out of our wallets and the ATM and then wondering at the end of the month where all the money has gone. You need to prevent that stress of living from paycheck to paycheck with no cushion to fall back on.

Take out a piece of paper or jump on your computer and start your Shopping Diet Log to document your monthly expenses. Use the following guidelines.

MONTHLY DEBT: WORK OUT WHAT YOU SPEND MONTHLY ON THE FOLLOWING ITEMS

Rent or Monthly Maintenance

Mortgage Payments

Credit Card Debt (don't forget to add your annual fees and any extra charges and divide by 12)

Car Loans

Student Loans

Utilities (e.g., water, electricity, gas, cable, TV, phone, Internet)

Monthly Transportation Expenses (e.g., subway, taxis, tolls, gas, rental cars)

Insurance Payments (e.g., car insurance, health insurance, life insurance, homeowner's insurance)

Membership Payments (e.g., gym, clubs, organizations)

Food (e.g., groceries, take-out, restaurants, coffee runs)

Regular Medical Expenses (e.g., prescriptions, medical equipment)

Income Taxes

Property Taxes

Accountants and/or Lawyers Fees (if you only use your accountant once a year, divide this payment by 12)

Regular Monthly Expenses for Children (e.g., tuition, babysitter, summer camp)

Regular Monthly Expenses for Pets (e.g., veterinarian bills, supplies, food, groomers)

Home Maintenance (e.g., gardener, housekeeper, cleaning products and supplies)

Personal Maintenance (e.g., haircuts, beauty regimens)

Entertainment (e.g., magazine subscriptions, concert tickets, season tickets to sports games)

Home Office Expenses (e.g., paper, printer ink, office supplies)

Retirement/Emergency Fund (e.g., savings for emergencies, IRA or 401K or other investments)

Luxuries (e.g., vacations, big-ticket splurges)

Remember to be very specific! Gum, cigarettes, magazines, and newspapers could be things that you buy on the fly, but you still consume them on a regular basis. Be sure to include these expenses—you'll be surprised at how the little things add up.

MONTHLY EARNINGS: WORK OUT WHAT COMES INTO YOUR HOUSEHOLD ON A MONTHLY BASIS

Monthly Income

Other Income (e.g., bonuses, stocks, freelance work, trust funds, rental property)

Income for Items You Sell (e.g., eBay, garage sales)

Bank Interest

Unexpected Income

Now, list your grand total and ask yourself: *How much goes in versus what goes out?* This chart will hopefully enlighten you in regard to what you can really afford to spend when shopping. The key is to stick to that number. It's as simple as keeping a shopping list (just like you should with groceries). This list is important and will prevent you from overspending. If there is a certain item you need or want that is too expensive for your budget, write it down and either wait for it to go on sale or find a creative way to cut back on your other expenses in order to save for it. Being resourceful will allow you to come up with creative economic solutions. Your Diet Log will become your money saver and lifesaver. You can't be accountable unless you start accounting for yourself and exactly what you're spending.

Based on your Diet Log, I want you to now calculate what your shopping threshold should be—how much you're allowed to spend without having to panic or experience buyer's remorse. Whenever I go shopping, I set a limit for myself. If I see something that I love and it's under my limit, it's a go. If it's over the amount, it's not always a *no,* but it's a *go slow.* I will think about the item and consider its real value to me. And, if I have forgotten about it after two or three days, it clearly wasn't that important to me after all. If the item is truly special, I will remember it, even write it down, keep tabs on it, and wait until it goes on sale. Sadly, there are times when some items will be gone before you can get to this point, and, like an ill-fated love affair, you must continue on with your fabulous life without the item of your dreams. However, I would rather lose it than have another inflated bill to pay and that sinking feeling of blowing my budget.

People have their own individual shopping threshold of what they can and cannot afford. No one wants to feel like they can't afford their own lives, but we also deserve a little

BLOCHBUSTER TIP

No one knows you better than you. So, if you feel too weak to go out into the field of dreams (the mall) without succumbing to spending, an easy money-saving solution is to leave your wallet (or at least the credit cards) at home. But remember to take your driver's license and any other IDs you need (because a ticket will be just another unnecessary expense you can't afford on your new budget!). Nothing will curb your appetite for shopping like having no access to your usual spending tools.

treat every now and then. With your new budget in mind and no bailouts in sight, let's finally go shopping.

What's in Store for You ⌣⌐

You wouldn't expect to find chili fries smothered in cheese at the Four Seasons. And you certainly wouldn't order a perfectly caramelized crème brûlée at the Olive Garden. Before you decide to eat at a restaurant, you pick one with the type of cuisine you're craving. You check out what kind of food is on the menu and how much it'll cost before you make a reservation. Well, the same idea is true for clothing stores. There are as many types of shops in the world as there are restaurants. They range from extremely exclusive and expensive to totally affordable. But in each one a *Shopping Diet* expert can find the tastiest of treats. You just have to make sure the place serves what you want. I'm letting you in on all the secret ingredients that make up every kind of store.

HIGH-END SPECIALTY DEPARTMENT STORES: Barneys, Neiman Marcus, Saks Fifth Avenue

These stores usually carry the best of the best in designer brand clothing, including collections from up-and-coming designers with cutting-edge styles. The hottest trends of the season, pulled directly from glossy fashion magazines, are always in stock. They can help any fashion novice dress like a fashionista. Most of these stores have a younger, hipper floor where you can get lower-priced designer brands. Their salespeople can act as your private stylists. This isn't just a job to them; it's their career. If they're up to par, they should know what works on different body types and can work within a range of budgets. These knowledgeable folks should help you put your most fashionable foot forward. Yes, the prices at these stores are higher, but it's the brand names, service, ambience, and exclusivity that you're paying for.

Tricks of the Trade: Specialty department stores—where the selection of designer goods is significantly larger than regular department stores—are known for their amazing seasonal sales, so keep track and make note of the dates. These shops are epicenters for the eclectic shoe shopper in particular. The real key here is to know your sales staff and make them work for you (without you having to pay them a weekly salary). They will also help when it comes to returns (but always hold on to receipts). These stores have exquisite tailoring departments to ensure that your couture creations fit like a glove. They usually also have a great restaurant in-house that always makes a day of shopping seem more like a grand event.

DEPARTMENT STORES: Macy's, Bloomingdales, Nordstrom

These stores have a wide range of brands and sizes, extremely flexible return policies, and lots of great sales. But the environments of department stores can vary and the merchandise might not always be unique. They're great places to buy sportswear items from big brands or special occasion dresses at affordable prices.

Tricks of the Trade: In these mega-fashion meccas, there is always a sale going on somewhere. Find a sales associate you like and make him or her your personal shopper. The people who work at department stores can clue you in about these sales and in-store promotions ahead of time. If you work together and build a relationship, they will let you know if they see something that would be perfect for you. If you treat them really well, they will even hold things for you before the big sale hits. Request garment bags and hangers—these are two things you shouldn't have to pay for. In addition, most stores offer complimentary basic alterations.

DESIGNER BOUTIQUES: Fred Segal, Jeffrey, Intermix, Scoop, Maxfield, Traffic

These stores are for the trendiest of the trendy. If it's not hip, happening, and hot, then you won't find it here. This is where designers' sartorial escapades are maximized for your viewing and shopping pleasure. Sales are few and far between. Most people simply come in just to look, become inspired, and probably get depressed when they see the price tags. (Make sure you bring your notebook with you. If you see something that you love and it's too expensive, write down the description—specifically the elements of the piece that you really love—to have a reference.) These days, it's easier to find something similar and less expensive at another, more affordable, store or a designer discount destination. The best part about designer boutiques is that they are extremely well edited and truly carry international and local designers you can't find elsewhere. They personify a precise and on-trend look that cannot help but serve as a source of inspiration.

Tricks of the Trade: Unless you are seriously thinking of

dropping a pretty penny to look pretty, the designer boutique may not be your shopping destination. There's no harm in browsing, though. Then you can run across the street to the safety of your favorite fashion outlet or fast fashion store to look for similar styles at a savvier price. The sales staff is supposed to be there to serve, yet they often need to be reminded of that fact. When these stores do have a sale, they are as subdued as the salespeople, whose attitudes can often be bigger than the discounts. And careful what you buy—once you spend money in these stores, it will stay there. When it comes to returns, not even the credit card companies can fight for you. Store credit is the best you'll get and usually only within two weeks of your purchase. Make sure to read return policies before you become entrapped in a bad retail romance.

VINTAGE STORES, CONSIGNMENT STORES, AND THRIFT SHOPS

Vintage stores offer one-of-a-kind items and great deals on used designer goods. And nowadays, the amount of time it takes for an item to be considered vintage is getting questionably shorter and shorter, so you never know what recent pieces you might find. However, sizes are limited, and the condition of an item can be an issue. But the unique pieces you find won't be on anyone else's back. A cute vintage dress or an antique coat with gorgeous buttons is a great way to express your individuality and eclectic sense of style. Usually, the items you purchase—from different periods of time and even different countries—quickly become conversation pieces. Everyone will want to know where they can get what you're wearing, but they won't be able to steal or emulate your personal style.

Tricks of the Trade: Prices are not set in stone, so consider bargaining with the seller, especially if you're buying multiple items. Your success will depend on the store: It'll be harder at a high-end emporium and much easier, even expected, at a flea market stall. Consignment or vintage does not always mean cheap: Price tags can still be astronomical depending on the garment, its history, and its designer. Be sure to look at the items in good lighting. Moth holes and old stains are often tricky to see until you get home and have the time to thoroughly inspect the item. These stores are great places to find unique accessories including jewelry, ties, purses, as well as exotic skins, most of which are often less expensive than if you bought them new. But return policies are usually incredibly stringent and most items are final sale, so let the buyer beware.

SPECIALTY CHAINS/FAST FASHION: Express, The Gap, TopShop, H&M, Zara, Forever 21

These stores know their customers and they have the market research to prove it. Once you find a brand that suits your style and body shape, you can count on finding many seasons of styles you love with a consistently good fit. (Each brand usually uses a specific fit model, so if one pair of their pants fit you, chances are, so will the rest.) They also manage to reflect trends without making their customers look like fashion victims. Some of these stores have even gotten on the designer bandwagon with high-end designer brands for a mere pittance of their normal cost. Specialty chains act as a hybrid between department stores and designer boutiques—while they offer a massive amount of inventory across a wide range of categories, each one caters to its specific niche and clientele. Some have even expanded to become more lifestyle oriented. The big downside is that often the clothing from these mass-market retailers is so ubiquitous that you can end up wearing the same clothes as all your friends . . . and too many strangers.

Tricks of the Trade: Things go on sale often—stay on top of price adjustments. If an item is reduced less than two weeks after you buy it, the store will usually refund you the difference. So keep all of those receipts. And stock in these stores move. The merchandise is as fresh as the bagels at the deli. Feel free to ask the sales associate when certain items will be reduced. Chances are the discount is right around the corner.

DISCOUNT STORES: Target, Walmart, JCPenney, Kohl's

The main thing these stores have going for them is their prices. Low prices, that is. They also offer quick, inexpensive interpretations of the latest trends in a wide range of sizes. The extremely affordable designer collaborations with discount stores have become as anticipated as fall's top fashion shows. Target may have started this trend with Isaac Mizrahi, Proenza Schouler, and Zac Posen, but other stores have quickly caught on. Kohl's features collections from Vera Wang and Daisy Fuentes while JCPenney carries lines by Bisou Bisou, Kimora Lee Simmons, and Charlotte Ronson. And

Sears has even made LL Cool J a designer! Because these stores seem so affordable, let the buyer beware: It's easy to overindulge. You might get caught up and end up with a pair of skinny jeans and an asymmetrical top, when you just went in for batteries. Don't give in to these impulse purchases—I've taught you better than that!

Tricks of the Trade: Stick to the basics. I mean it. Make a list if you have to. Try not to get too distracted by the bells, whistles, and other forms of marketing noise that seem to be playing just for you in discount stores. After all, you don't want to get caught up in wearing the emperor's new clothes, even if they were discounted.

DESIGNER OUTLET STORES: Tanger Outlet Mall, Loehmann's, Filene's Basement, Daffy's, DSW, Annie Sez

You have to enter discount stores, such as Loehmann's, Century 21, Marshalls, and my favorites, Tanger Outlet Mall and DSW, with an open mind. Perfect for high-end essentials at a lower price point, they carry everything from the most famous designer labels to the most obscure. But if you're looking for something extremely specific, your time might be better spent at a department store (though you will spend more money). I love to think of discount outlets like Las Vegas: You gotta get lucky. If you're open to a wide variety of items and designer labels at an extremely discounted price, then an outlet is a great way to throw caution to the wind and explore the racks.

Tricks of the Trade: Always check the quality of the item that has piqued your interest. Beware of the smallest imperfections. Are there any rips? Is the material pilled? Does the zipper work? Are there any missing buttons? Or stains in obscure places? Remember, clothing hits the discount stores for a reason. What should be considered damaged beyond repair? Pass on rips and tears unless you truly love the piece. If the tear is in a seam, it can be easily mended by a tailor. A missing button isn't a tragedy. You can sew on new buttons and have a piece that looks as good as new. Look for what is missing on an item. You don't want that khaki trench coat that's missing a belt. Even if it is only $35, it will never look right with this key part missing. But, if the coat is too long and needs hemming, let it join the fix-it pile in your own closet boutique. You can use that extra fabric to make a belt. Pay close attention to the discounts offered on an item. Many times, a piece of clothing will be marked 40 percent off, but it's on a rack that promises another 10 percent discount. Never be embarrassed to ask clerks if you're entitled to the additional discount (or have them double-check if they simply give you a shrug). After all, you're here to get the best bargain possible. Basic coats are a great buy at discount outlets. If you're in the market for a simple midlength wool coat for winter or a spring slicker, then you can't go wrong when they're often more than half off. Even in designer outlets, an item that you love may be out of your price range. Don't get upset. A hefty price tag is a hefty price tag, no matter where it's located. However, if you do find something at an outlet that you love and it's the right price, buy it that day. You probably won't see it again if you wait. These stores are all about moving their stock.

THE INTERNET: eBay.com, Shopbop.com, OneStopPlus.com

The Internet is probably the best place in the world to find bargains. You can search for an item across multiple websites to compare prices or bid for an item on eBay. And Internet-only stores do not charge sales tax. The only bummer is that you don't get to touch anything, much less try it on before you buy it. And while most websites have liberal return policies, shipping to and fro can be a pain, not to mention expensive and time-consuming.

Tricks of the Trade: Let's say you find a dress that you love at a local store, but it's too expensive. Try it on anyway. Write down the description, size, style number, and color in your shopping notebook. Then check for a better price in the same exact style online. You may be able to save a bundle, and you know you're safe from an annoying return because you've done your research. Don't forget to check the websites for department stores, which often offer specific promotions for online shoppers as well as different inventory than what you would find on their retail floor. And don't be afraid to ask if shipping is covered by the company. Recently, one of my plus-size clients turned me onto an amazing online store called OneStopPlus (www.onestopplus.com). The variety on this site for the curvaceous consumer is astounding. Whether you are a plus-size exec, trend follower, or stay-at-home mom, this site has clothing in sizes 14 to 44 that you'll love. (They even have clothes for big and tall men.)

As we all know, the Internet can be very addictive, so it's important to put a time limit on your online shopping. Time is money, and you might be wasting more than you're saving.

You might also be spending more money than you should! The click of the mouse can be too easy. Always beware of impulse buying, late-night shopping sprees, and depression spending that can push you and your credit card debt further over the edge.

CATALOGS: L.L. Bean, J.Crew, dELiA*s, Anthropologie

Catalogs are like globe-trotting friends: They find obscure things from far-flung places. And they usually carry special sizes and offer very liberal return policies. They share the same fit and shipping issues with web stores, although they do have live customer service representatives available by phone in case you need help figuring out your size—they will often be able to provide you with specific measurements. The great thing about catalogs is that you can shop at home and you don't have to be computer literate to use them. Many catalogs work in tandem with the Internet, so you can place your orders by phone or computer.

Tricks of the Trade: If you're making friends with a customer service representative at a catalog company, chances are that you're using them too much. But if you do manage to make a connection with a nice phone rep over the phone lines, this person can give you secret discounts, waive shipping fees, and locate hard-to-find items. Though catalogs have become less relevant in the fashion industry thanks to the Internet, the home decorating industry seems to have taken hold of the medium and made it its own (e.g., Ikea, Restoration Hardware, Pottery Barn, and West Elm).

TELEVISION: QVC, HSN

TV is a tricky place to shop. If you insist on mixing your remote control with your credit card control, please be very, very careful. Just calling one of those 800 numbers often means you'll receive a shipment of face cream every month whether you like it or not. That said, some celebrity brands and interesting gadget-type items are only available on television and occasionally offer good values. Television is an excellent source for storage, cleaning, and organizational items as well. QVC and HSN have upped their fashion ante with collections from designers like Randolphe Duke, Tina Knowles, Diane von Furstenberg, and even Patricia Field. These networks also have stringent quality control. Just be careful not to let a boring evening vegging out on the couch turn into months of budgetary mayhem.

Tricks of the Trade: My advice with television purchases is to step away from the phone, turn off the TV, and put down the

BLOCH**BUSTER** TIP

When it comes to shopping over the Internet, television, or via catalogs, be aware of inevitable shipping and handling charges. Often items will be shipped separately and you will incur each individual charge. That can add up to a big and surprising dollar amount. Make sure to ask about shipping and handling before you make your purchase, and feel free to negotiate alternative shipping solutions.

remote. Yes, you read right. If there is something you decide you can't live without after the first flush from those gamma rays are gone, the item can usually be found on the shopping network's website. Yes, there's a chance it will be sold out. But even if it is, most likely they will bring the item back, often at a discount, before the designer's next appearance on the show.

Shop Smart

I shop for a living. When I first started out in my career, I made a lot of mistakes that resulted in frantic trips in search of items or throwing myself at the mercy of a salesperson as I pleaded my case for why the store should accept a return without a receipt. And let's not even talk about some of the crazy trends that I got caught up in. Those fashion faux pas proved invaluable. I learned the most important tips and tricks to make shopping not only easy but also enjoyable. Now I'm letting you in on the secrets of a professional shopper.

DRESS FOR SUCCESS

When dressing for your shopping excursion, look pretty, but be practical. Leave your heavy coat at home, wear versatile undergarments, and choose easy-off clothes and flat slip-on shoes. (Bring heels if you are shopping for something that will be worn with them.) You don't want to exhaust yourself as you try on clothes. If you struggle with the outfit you're wearing, you'll either give up out of frustration or buy something hastily that you'll later regret.

NOT A FAMILY AFFAIR

Don't shop with a begrudging husband, a nagging mother, or a child who has no patience. Do you think Angelina Jolie packs up her brood every time she goes on a shopping spree? Hell no! Take a friend who will enjoy a day out and will give you good advice on your buys.

MAKE A FRIEND

Salespeople want to feel useful, so make them your own personal stylists. They will tell you when your bottom looks too big in those pants. Beg them to be honest with you—a happy customer will be a consistent customer. They will also give you the inside scoop on which labels run small (or big). They can even pull the best from new shipments before they hit the floor. Just be sure to hook up with someone whose style you respect. If they can't help themselves, how can they help you?

POWER SHOP

If you can get all of your shopping done in an hour—fantastic—but don't expect that every time. If you've got a wedding to go to, don't go shopping the morning of the event for that perfect thing to wear. Give everything its appropriate amount of time and effort. You work hard for your money. Don't throw it away on pressured purchases. Budget your time as well as you budget your funds.

PHILLIP BLOCH

SHOPPING ABROAD

When I go traveling, I love to visit foreign department stores and buy something nobody will have at home. But make sure you are crystal clear on foreign exchange rates! Clothes can make for unique and useful souvenirs (as opposed to that cheesy T-shirt or magnet that just collects dust). These items will truly contribute to your own sense of style and remind you of your wonderful trip every time you put them on. The world is your oyster—use it as your style inspiration. Remember when you are abroad to always ask for the de-tax papers. You are entitled to a tax break, so why not get the refund you deserve? Most foreign stores have the paperwork to fill out to get all that extra tax money back. It may take a few extra moments, but the savings can be substantial—often upward of 18 percent. If you are buying five items, it's almost like getting one of them for free (in fashionomics, anyway!). Make sure to read the rules and don't forget to hand the paperwork over at the airport before you head home. If you are using a credit card abroad, beware of exchange rates or penalties your credit card may charge you.

WRAP IT UP

When shopping at department stores or boutiques, have your purchases gift wrapped. Many stores offer this as a complimentary service (especially at holiday time). Everything you buy will be a gift to yourself. Plus you can reuse and recycle those boxes, bags, and bows to keep the gift of giving going. I also find that leaving the tags on something that you bought out of season until you can wear it will keep the item feeling like new. That cashmere sweater you bought in July will be like an early holiday gift to yourself when you break it out in November.

MAKE A DAY OF IT

Budget some time to have lunch in the store's cafe or a favorite nearby eatery. But that doesn't mean you should skip breakfast. Just as you shouldn't grocery shop on an empty stomach, you shouldn't clothing shop on one, either. You'll get cranky pretty quickly. If you do plan a lunch in the middle of your shopping excursion, don't gorge—just graze. Otherwise, you'll feel bloated and bad about yourself and the clothes you are trying on.

All About Clothes

You need to address the following issues when shopping specifically for clothing.

THE BEST BANG FOR YOUR BUCK

Always look for clothes that you can wear in different ways. For example, if you find a wonderful cashmere sweater with a gorgeous satin belt, you can use that belt with the sweater or with another piece such as a dress or a pair of pants or even as a headband. You can look at that type of purchase as a twofer and justify spending a little more money since you'll wear it more often. Now that's a shop-ortunity!

HERD MENTALITY

One of the biggest mistakes rookie shoppers make is to ignore racks with many of the same skirts, shirts, pants, or dresses hung together. It gives them the feeling that these items aren't special and every woman on the street will be wearing them. Look past the way a store has displayed its products—you can't assess how many of a particular style exists this way. Some shops might only put out a few dresses to give an impression of exclusivity; meanwhile, there are dozens of the same style in the back room. (That's why if you don't find the size you are looking for on the floor, always ask a salesperson to check if it's in stock in their store or in stock at another of the store's locations. If the latter is the case, the store will usually be able to ship it to you or your local location free of charge.)

EMBELLISHMENTS

Dresses and shirts with a lot of embellishments, such as big stones, sparkling crystals, or metal studs, are an easy way to create an instant and memorable outfit. These pieces are a fabulous fashion fix if you never have enough time or don't feel you have the natural knowledge to accessorize your ensemble. A few well-chosen items in your wardrobe will give you a finished look without much effort. However, you shouldn't wear these stylized items as staples because they're just too recognizable. Use them sparingly as wardrobe statements. If you're on a limited financial budget but possess a lot of creativity, skip these pieces and embellish simpler styles with your own collection of jewelry or belts.

FOR THE FASHION NOVICES

If you're the type of woman who likes to throw something on and then run out of the house, buy those embellished dresses or shirts. In this case, embellished pieces are a fabulous fashion fix if you never have enough time or don't feel you have the natural knowledge to accessorize your ensemble. A few well-chosen items in your wardrobe will give you a finished look without much effort. For the creative consumer, this type of clothing can seem stifling because there's not much room for change or personal style.

WATCH OUT FOR RETRO

I know that Marcia Brady red A-line 1970s-style dress in the department store seems cute, but do you want to be one of the twenty Marcia, Marcia, Marcias on the street? If you are going retro, head to the local vintage store where, for a fraction of the cost, you can find an original mod dress that no one else is wearing. But double-check before you seal the deal on the dress that it doesn't make you look like you're headed to a costume party.

BASIC SAVINGS

When buying basics, a great way to save money is by choosing the department store's in-house brands. Every store usually manufactures their eponymous brand merchandise in the same factory as more expensive designer labels. That means they offer the same quality and look. While many stores use their own name on the label, some might not be as obvious. Some stores like to disguise their own lines with a different label among their branded merchandise, so don't be afraid to ask a sales rep the name of the store's own line.

SALES ALERT

Take advantage when your favorite department store puts classic items such as camisoles, cardigans, turtlenecks, or tees on sale. They usually come in a variety of colors and are great wardrobe fillers for those whose closets need a bit of nourishment. These smaller pieces are invaluable to stretching your wardrobe. You can put that simple red tank under a suit during the week and then wear it with shorts on a hot summer weekend. But you don't need to pay full price. Just keep your eye on the sales.

LACY THINGS

Lace shirts are romantic and feminine, but you don't need ten of them. One or two will suffice for this statement piece. I always get questioned about how to wear them. It's simple: Put a nude tank or a color-coordinated camisole underneath the lacy item (wearing a bra alone is usually baring a bit too much).

DAZED AND CONFUSED

If a shirt or a dress has too many colors or too many things going on at once, then it's clearly in the midst of its own identity crisis. If it's causing too much confusion just to look at it, it's best to put it back on the rack. Patterns are not for the fashion faint of heart.

DAMAGED GOODS

If you pick out a piece and it's damaged, don't get disappointed. It can mean more savings for you. A missing button that costs a dollar to replace could save you twenty. Usually, a salesperson isn't authorized to reduce the price, but a manager is. Gently ask a salesperson to speak to a manager. Then show the manager the defect and simply ask what kind of discount he or she can give. Don't be shy to save on a buy!

DO YOUR HOMEWORK

If you love designers, then read fashion magazines to see what they're up to each season. Try on some of their pieces (even if you don't have the funds or occasion to make a purchase) in order to check out the various cuts. The point is to figure out which designers create clothes that work best for your body type. When you eventually do have a special event or the money in the bank for a splurge, it won't be an overwhelming experience to find your designer dream. You'll already know that Catherine Malandrino dresses or BCBG pants fit your body best.

WEAR AND RETURN

I know most fashionistas have worn clothes and returned them to stores at least once in their lives, but this practice is not a good idea. First of all, it's unethical. Stores aren't in business to loan clothes. They are there to sell! Plus, if you get a stain on your "loaner," consider it sold.

WRINKLE TEST

Before you buy an item, give it the wrinkle test. Crinkle the fabric in your hand for about ten seconds to see if it will crease easily. If it's wrinkled after seconds in your hand, imagine how it will look after a half hour at the office. Many love linen and silk, but wear it once and you'll be more wrinkled than your neighbor's shar-pei!

PANTS PERFECT

Make sure the butt area of your pants fits well. It is the hardest area to alter. Even the savviest tailor has a hard time restructuring it. You can always take in the waist, but taking in the thighs presents a lot of serious problems. The pants will never fit right again. Always pass on those items that don't fit right in that zone.

RIGHT SIZE

Everyone's true size is unique to them. That's why you are a size 6 in some stores and a size 10 in others. Or you wear a 12

BLOCHBUSTER TIP

For years, the iron was our only best friend to get out those pesky wrinkles. But these days, I suggest using handheld steamers. They're convenient, easy to use, highly portable, and quite precise. Rowenta is the brand that I carry in my Stylist Kit.

on the top but a 16 on the bottom. It's enough to make you get out a calculator. It's particularly important to know your two distinct sizes on top and bottom—often, they are not the same. Suits or two-piece bathing suits may be difficult to find because you will need two different sizes or will have to have extreme alterations to compensate. I recommend getting measured once by a tailor so that you know the size of every important point, especially the neck, waist, breast, and sleeve length. Having these measurements will make it easier to shop for clothes in any store and especially online.

TRY IT ON!

This may sound basic, but I can't reinforce it enough. Always, and I do mean always, try on clothes before you buy them. Look at yourself in the mirror, keeping in mind the twelve zones of your body and the work you did in the mirror at home. Now you have learned to trust your reflection. If what sticks in your mind is a negative, don't try to justify the reaction. You don't have to overanalyze why something you like doesn't look good on you. Just hang it back on the rack and move on. You have the knowledge and tools to shop without doubt.

How to Shop While Shedding Pounds

People often ask me how to maintain a sense of style while losing weight. It's a tricky issue. As your size shrinks, you don't want to be left with lots of clothes you can no longer wear. However, if you are dieting in a healthy way, it might take a while to get to your ideal weight. And you don't want to look like a frump the entire time. Here's what to do on your way to a slimmer you.

* Go for knits and jersey material, but make sure the items are not too loose or tight-fitting.

* A button shirt is a good option, especially if there is stretch built into the fabric. But pay attention to puckering at the button placket—if it's pulling and doesn't lay smooth, your shirt is too tight. Once you lose weight, the button shirt might fit a little looser, but it's still a chic alternative to a fitted look.

* You should buy pants and skirts that are nonconfining and fit comfortably. Try elastic waists or drawstrings. You will get more fashion mileage out of these pieces because they will continue to adjust along with

your changing weight and body shape. I'm not talking about sweatpants here. Losing weight can be a trying experience, so you need clothes that will give you a boost. There are lots of nice-looking, even dressy, pant styles with elastic or drawstring waists.

* Empire waists and A-line shapes are terrific for skirts and dresses. Tunic tops and peasant dresses are great solutions as well. These styles will likely still fit you when you lose the weight.

* A little stretch built right into a garment is worth its weight in gold. These pieces fit just right without making you look like you've been stuffed into your outfit. They also give you flexibility while still looking sexy.

* Jackets are hard to buy when losing weight. Cardigans work the best because a knit will adapt to your changing weight. If you need to wear jackets or blazers for work, buy a classic Chanel-style or a shirt-style jacket, both of which aren't meant to be closed or fitted. Or you could try a looser style with a belt to accentuate your waist.

* If you're trying to lose a few pounds and need to get something new to wear, go shopping at stores like H&M and Zara, because you don't want to spend a lot of money on clothes that won't fit you in a few seasons. However, these stores are definitely geared

toward the tinier and the trendier. For plus-size ladies, stores like Target, JCPenney, Kohl's, Old Navy, and Victoria's Secret are where you should do the bulk of your shopping. You get a lot of style for a small price in a bigger size until those pounds melt away.

✻ If you must buy a pair of jeans in this awkward stage of losing weight, try Lee Denim, J.Crew, The Gap, or anywhere that sells Levi's. Don't spend big bucks on jeans at this point.

✻ To lose weight and keep it off, it must be done right. It is not something to be done in a hurry. But if you do need a quick slimming fix, pick up Maidenform's Flexees Fat-Free Dressing solutions. My clients love this stuff! You can also try Hanes Smooth Illusions, Leggs Profiles for a great buy, or even Spanx.

✻ Make sure the clothes you buy actually fit you. If you're a size 12, don't buy size 10 pants. Nothing looks worse than a cheap pair of pants that don't fit right. If they're snug, fine—but you don't want those pants to be pulling at the thighs. Just say no to camel toe.

Working the Sales

I know, I know. We all love a sale. There's something about that four-letter word that immediately quickens the pulse and sends a thrill through our systems. Yes, getting something

> ## BLOCHBUSTER TIP
>
>
> Heavier people tend to wear oversized clothing, believing that this will cover up their weight. In reality, these clothes actually make you look bigger. If you are full-figured and curvy, tailored and more fitted (but not too tight!) clothing can highlight your shape and make you look even sexier.

wonderful for less than full price is, well, wonderful. But a sale does not necessarily equal a bargain or even good economic sense. Case in point: If you can get three neon midriff-baring shirts for the price of two, you are still left with three tacky shirts too many. So let's see how to make the most of your money.

✳ It's a smart idea to keep tabs on when your favorite stores are having sales. But even if you decide to shop while there isn't a storewide sale, keep your eye out for a sales rack or two hiding somewhere. And always watch for special promotions. Most stores offer 10 to 15 percent off your first day's purchases if you open a store credit card—but let the buyer beware: You could just be opening up another way to increase your debt. I suggest that you save this trick of the trade for specific sprees like back-to-school shopping or for big-ticket purchases. Use it for that one-time purchase, get the savings, and then hide or cut up the card.

❋ Most major department stores offer lots of different deals with their own credit cards. Many times, you can earn points for every dollar you spend in the store. At the end of the year, these points accumulate and you end up receiving gift cards. I save those cards until the big seasonal sale for that extra big bonus bargain. There are even specific shopping days when you can earn double points for every dollar you spend. I use my Barneys and Saks credit card points to score decadent designer deals. Often, when you use your department store credit card at one of their outlet locations, you can get an even deeper discount. I love when a department store creates a promotion where the more you buy the more you get back. If you purchase $100 in merchandise, you can get another $50 worth of goods for free. (It's fun, but don't buy things you don't need just because it allows you to get more.) If you've been eyeing a dress or new suit, buy it on one of those special days.

❋ Until fairly recently, sample sales were only open to fashion insiders. But over the last few years, they have become public domain and are cropping up in more and more places. Sample sales are basically a chance for a designer or store to sell off their excess stock. The items are usually from the current season but are offered at a fraction of the price. The sales run for a very limited time—often during a weekend—and the lines to get in can be crazy. But so can the savings! Resist the temptation to shop by mob mentality. Just because some women are grabbing items like maniacs (and they definitely will be

DESIGNER DIVISION

Always take note when high-priced designer clothing items go on sale, particularly when those items are staple wardrobe pieces. Maybe it's a new Dolce & Gabbana suit that will replace your five-year-old bruised and battered one. In these situations, I suggest using Designer Division, a formula I invented to create a space for you to really think about and estimate fashion's true value. If the suit originally cost $2,600 and it's now 40 percent off, that brings the suit to $1,560. You'll probably have the suit for the same five years that you had the last one, wearing all the pieces together once a week and as separates another two times a week. That's three times a week that the suit will be in use. If you work it out, you'll wear the suit 156 times a year . . . and 780 times in five years. As a result, you will essentially be spending $2 every time you wear the suit. Now, that's a good investment!

doing that) doesn't mean what they're snatching is worth your dollars. Be judicious like you would anywhere else. The only difference from a typical shopping experience is that normally there aren't any dressing rooms at sample sales. So you either have to flash a little skin in public or take a chance that the item will fit. It's a bit like fashion roulette: no risk, no savings, no reward. See the shopping directory on page 217 for more details.

✳ Always look online and in your local newspaper for sales happening at your favorite stores. As mentioned previously, it helps to befriend salespeople and ask them to call or email you when a specific item goes on sale. That's the best: getting something on sale that you know you want.

> ## BLOCHBUSTER TIP
>
> Just like rising and falling hemlines, taxes are inevitable and should be factored into your shopping diet. You can pay anywhere from 7 to 30 percent on your purchases. Never look at the price tag on a piece of clothing as the price you will be paying—always factor in the tax before you head to the cashier to save you the surprise when you see your total. Keep in mind that some states offer tax-free days as incentives to go out and buy. Mark these on your calendar, especially if you're planning on making any big purchases. Look into the sales tax rules and regulations of your state and make a note of the perks . . . and the drawbacks. That's also true when traveling: You don't want that souvenir to cost the same as your airfare home!

All About Shoes

There's no business like shoe business. So, attention shoppers: I know that many of you have had a lifelong affair with shoes. You might be thrilled to own those snakeskin platform booties. But you'll fall off your heels when you receive your credit card bill and realize you have to live on Ramen noodles to pay it off. (No shoes, no matter how gorgeous, are worth that level of MSG intake.) It's time to deal with the addiction so that it is no longer an affliction.

When it comes to your shoe wardrobe, always consider form, function, comfort, and uniqueness before you plunk down that card. Do you really need strappy sandals in this summer's hot color for $250? Now that you're on *The Shopping Diet,* take a pass. A big money splurge on the trends or the hottest colors of any given season is not smart. If you love a pair of shoes that are trendy, write down their description and see if you can match the expensive pair with a lesser-known brand or a pair that is similar in look.

If you're going to invest big money on shoes, go for a basic pair that pays big attention to small details. A black pump with a comfortable kitten heel in gold is the kind of thing I'm talking about. That style of shoe is not only classic and can go with numerous outfits, but it also features a bold detail that makes it worth the extra splurge. Your job is to look for shoes

---

BLOCHBUSTER TIP

I recommend DSW for clients who are looking to get more for less. Take the inspirational ideas and designer names from your notebook, and I'm sure you'll find many of them present and accounted for at DSW.

that are versatile yet special. I would never tell you to buy $600 basic black pumps. You can find the basic pump in any shoe store at every price.

My other major rule regarding shoes—and I will shout it from the highest clothing rack—is that you should never, ever buy any shoe that kills your feet. Scratch that. You shouldn't even buy shoes that hurt your feet a little bit. There's no need to suffer for beauty. If the shoe pinches or you feel your toe aching and you've only done one round through the shoe department, then this is the wrong shoe for you. We've all purchased those gorgeous shoes that hurt, thinking they will miraculously be comfortable later. And we all know the end of that story. After one bloody and blistered evening, we never wear those shoes again. You don't need another shoe box gathering dust in your newly cleaned-out closet. Remember, when you are trying on shoes, mimic how you will wear that shoe. If you are planning to wear a pair without socks, then try the shoes on without socks. And also consider that your feet are always a little more swollen in the afternoon than in the morning. Though your weight may fluctuate, your shoe size will usually stay about the same.

WAKE-UP CALL

If you are the kind of person who buys shoes in the price range of your rent, consider this: That $400 you shelled out for stilettos is the cost of a weekend trip or many dinners with friends. What would you rather own—shoes that are in for a season or memories that last a lifetime?

IF THE SHOE FITS

I've dealt with every shoe out there—from a strappy sandal for a starlet who'll be strutting her stuff down the red carpet for hours to a knockoff of a $900 shoe for a good friend. Here are my golden rules for what goes on your feet.

* Spend a little extra and buy gels and pads to make shoes more comfortable. They also make shoes last longer. The inside of your shoe will always look pristine and clean. Dr. Scholl's has a great variety of affordable solutions.

* Always weatherproof your shoes before you wear them. It's only a few dollars to protect your investment. Just because you think you will never wear your pumps in the snow does not mean it won't snow while you're wearing them.

* Don't go for the trend du jour when buying expensive shoes. Big-ticket shoe items should be classic with a little designer edge that wouldn't be replicable in a cheaper version.

* When buying heels, opt for a reasonable heel height that works for you. Don't be ambitious, because you'll wear shoes more when you can actually be comfortable in them.

✻ If you really want a trendy look, then buy the cheaper version, because chances are, you will probably only wear it for one season. Nowadays, trends are knocked off more and more rapidly. A copy of the Balenciaga gladiator pump was sold at Strawberry about two weeks after it debuted at Barneys. These trend-driven replicas are easy to find and last about as long as the trend itself.

✻ Don't buy what I call closet collector's pieces. Yes, those gold lamé pumps with the sequins look sparkly and gorgeous under the bright store lights. But stop, breathe, and ask: Truthfully, how many times do you even go out at night? And they're very high heels, so you probably won't even be able to walk farther than from the car to the restaurant. If you don't have a limo in your life, these creations don't fit your lifestyle.

✻ Don't make your feet a walking advertisement. I don't mind if the shoes are clearly designer, but not vulgar designer. Decide which category that big logo falls into before you buy.

✻ You hate those boring black flats? Add two matching pins to the front. This is a chic-onomics tip to embellish any shoe. You can also buy fancy rhinestone clip-on earrings and instantly take a shoe from blah to *wow*!

✻ Check the entire shoe before you buy it to make sure there aren't any construction problems. If you see beginning signs of breakage, forget it. If the straps look like they're two quick laps away from giving out, then pass. There is nothing worse than spending money on a product that is defective from day one.

* When it comes to sandals, make sure you don't have toe spillage. Your toes need to stay in your shoes.

* Avoid the seven dwarves of shoes: too clunky, too high, too flat, too pointy, too embellished, too cheap, or too expensive.

* Check the ankle straps to make sure they're not cutting you in the wrong place to make your leg look shorter and wider. If you're not sure, just walk away.

* If the shoes feel slightly tight, you can take them to the shoe repairman to get them stretched out and usually gain half a size. But don't buy shoes thinking they will fit better if you get them stretched. If they feel too tight or are uncomfortable in any way in the store, chances are that stretching them a half size is *not* going to do the trick.

SHOE PROBLEMS AND SOLUTIONS

People are obsessed with shoes. I'm constantly getting asked questions about materials, prices, blisters—you name it. I thought I would share a few helpful answers with you.

GETTING HIGH

A five-inch heel isn't everyone's thing. And that's okay. There's no problem with deciding that two inches is your limit. No matter your height, choose a heel that you can walk and stand in comfortably. Go with a wider heel or wedge if you can't stand standing on spikes. Just like with clothes, it's a matter of trying things on and figuring out what works best for you. While you're on any shoe expedition, do a little homework. Try on some heels in various heights to find the right altitude. The kitten heel is a great standby because most people can wear it, and it still gives a sexy lift. In the end, three comfortable inches are better than five painful ones.

Q: Should I buy those classic designer brown sling backs for $300? I know that I will wear them to death and they go with everything I own.

A: I know they seem like a good buy because you will get a lot of use out of them, but put the expensive sling backs down, step away, and think about it. You can actually get the same look for less. There is no need to bring out the big bucks when it comes to buying the basics. What's practical should be affordable.

Q: I'm in lust with these $450 black patent leather flats with big gold buckles on the front. Should I buy them? They have a very unique designer detail.

A: Put that buckle shoe back on the rack. You can buy a cheaper pair of basic black leather flats *anywhere,* then go to a fabric store and purchase two buckles for about $10. For an additional $30, a good shoemaker can sew those buckles on. Now, let's add this up: You could have purchased those $450 buckle flats. Instead, you found $40 simple flats at Nine West. Then you spent $10 on buckles and $30 on the work. Now you are ready to put your most fashionable foot forward for under $100.

Q: I'm a bridesmaid and I have to buy my own shoes. Any advice?

A: I would be loath to spend a lot on a shoe that can only be worn to formal events. This is a great time to cheap out. If you have to buy a shoe in a highly specific color, go for the dye-ables. Almost any shoe store, bridal store, or online bridal website has a great assortment. Buy a comfortable and classic white shoe and dye it to match. You can always visit your fashion ally, the shoemaker, and redye it to a more sensible color after the wedding. (Remember, when dyeing, you can always dye to a darker color but never to a lighter one.) Another great option is the basic silver or gold strappy sandal, which goes with every color under the sun (even that horrible lime green bridesmaid's dress your friend picked out). These shoes instantly say "formal," but in your everyday life, they can transform a pair of jeans into a chic nighttime look.

Q: I hate heels, so I walk around all day in nothing but black leather ballet flats. Since these are my main shoes, can I splurge and buy the very best?

A: This is like asking: Is it better to spend $4 on a McDonald's hamburger or spend $120 on a Royale from the pricey Manhattan eatery DB Bistro Moderne? Guess what? It's still a ground beef patty between two pieces of bread. Don't fall into a fashion rut. Take the money you want to spend on higher-end flats and put them toward a wedge or kitten heel. Both are equally as comfortable as a flat but give an extra chic edge. If a black flat is your shoe of choice, then buy a midrange pair in a soft leather for $100. And make sure the flats are comfortable since this seems to be your modus operandi. Or even try them in a patent or a classic dark color other than black for a change of pace. But there is certainly no need to purchase a pair that costs $400 and up.

Q: I have my eye on a fabulous pair of menswear-inspired white and black patent leather spectator pumps that are a work of art, yet so comfortable. They are out of my budget, but I want to find a way to buy them responsibly. I'm ready to sacrifice for these beauties. Help!

A: I applaud your willingness to save in another aspect of your life for something you really value. The fact that you are going to sacrifice in order to acquire these shoes will make you appreciate them even more. If you are like a lot of women I know, you probably spend at least three or four dollars a day on lattes, frappuccinos, or mochas. Vow to give up your expensive (and probably caloric) caffeine fix until you've saved up the equivalent for your spectator pumps. If coffee isn't your poison, find another expense of equal value that you can forgo. These shoes are unique and worth saving to own. But don't make them a staple shoe that you'll wear a few times a week, or they'll get old and worn out fast. Enjoy them, but wear them sparingly to make them last longer.

$Q:$ I have a pair of leather booties that I just love, but they give me blisters in one spot. Is there anything I can do?

$A:$ My friend turned me onto the best product for blister prevention: BAND-AID Brand ACTIV-FLEX BLISTER BLOCK STICK. It's similar to rub-on deodorant for your feet. Rub this clear stick on your feet before strutting your stuff and you should be blister-free.

All About Bags

There is really no rhyme or reason to bag pricing these days. The smallest miniaudiere could cost you as much as a down payment on a home while the largest hobo bag could be well within your budget. You could spend $30,000 on a Hermès Kelly Bag . . . or buy a car for the same amount! Prices on designer bags are not based on the amount of detail or the quality of the product. The designer label and the mystique of the brand is what make a certain bag more or less expensive. And let's face it, the bag of the moment changes quicker than the interest rates on your credit card. A purse can often go out of style before you're out of its debt.

Don't fall into this marketing trap. When buying a bag, particularly a leather one, pay special attention to how it feels. Go for something that is neither too soft nor too hard—this will make it less likely to crack or rip. Check the stitching and pull on the parts. Give that purse a test drive before you own it. Make sure it can hold weight. Will those straps break easily? Are they reinforced? Is the lining strong? Play with the hardware on the bag (silver, brass, or nickel lasts the longest). The buckles must not be heavier than the material. If so, the buckle will pull away from the purse. Make sure the zipper isn't hard to use and the tab isn't going to break off. You know how rough your life can be on you. Make sure your bag can keep up.

On a diet, we sometimes pop in that little piece of candy for a tiny sugar rush—do the same on your *Shopping Diet*. If you have a little more room to splurge and add to your trusty leather bag, I always recommend buying a bag in a pop color for that little extra piece of eye candy. It punctuates an outfit. But beware of light and pastel colors—they show pen stains and scuff marks quickly and easily, especially on the bottom. It helps to pay attention to where you're setting your bag down, no matter the color of the purse. Those germs could be with you longer than your bag! I encourage my clients to pretreat their bags with stain-resistant sprays to extend their average life expectancy.

Bags in exotic skins are another great way to bring out an outfit's wild side. But these skins are a costly feature. Luckily, they are easily duplicated these days in leather or vinyl. And most people can't tell what's real and what's faux unless it jumps up and bites them—and an exotic animal doesn't have to be killed. Textured or patent leathers are also great because they don't show as much wear as real skin.

It's not just about the outside but what's on the inside that counts when considering your bag. Dark linings are much better because they show less wear and dirt. You should always spray the inside of the bag as well so that it, too, is stain and liquid resistant. They say that M&Ms melt in your mouth and not in your hands. Well, they'll also melt in your bag. You can preserve the interior of your bag by using water-proof pouches to help separate and organize its contents. Use a plastic makeup bag or pouch inside your purse for your wallet and phone. (You'll never have to dump your purse out to find your phone again!) Use another waterproof pouch for any liquids, lotions, and potions so that they won't get all over your wallet and checkbook if they break or leak. What else do you need when you're in a hurry? Your keys? Your contact lens solution? Your pen? Create a special pouch for these essential items. If you color code your pouches, they'll be even easier to spot and pull out in a hurry.

If dogs are a man's best friend, well, then, bags are a lady's. Here's how to get your perfect purse.

BLOCHBUSTER TIP

Twice a year, vow to clean out all of your purses to get rid of that excess gunk and junk that has sunk to the bottom. Toss out all of the needless things that have built up over the last six months. You don't need those dirty tissues or old chewing gum. Make sure to get all the loose change and put it into a piggy bank. You'll be surprised how quickly it'll fill up. Your back will also thank you for removing all that excess weight.

EVENING BAGS

When it comes to evening bags, I love inexpensive vintage ones that give you a lot of dazzle for your dollar. Look for beading and embellishments that make them stand out. Be sure to check out the condition of the bag in good lighting. Vintage bags have endured years of wear and tear that might not be easily visible in the ambience of the store. You shouldn't spend a lot on evening bags because you won't use them very often. Macy's and Aldo are good shops for inexpensive clutches, especially if you can't afford time sifting through vintage stores. If you already have a plain satin bag, you can add a sparkling pin for a fun and festive variation.

OVERSIZED BAGS

Big bags are a mainstay of the fashionable set, but they can kill your back. So if you choose to lug around a bag that's half your size, please don't fill it up. Large bags are certainly multi-functional and can double as a day bag, gym bag, book bag, computer bag, or chic carryall for your next weekend trip. I love the look, luxury, and practicality of a big bag, but if there's too much stuff in there, you won't be able to find a thing. I recommend taking a clutch, filling it with your essentials (your wallet, keys, phone, etc.), and throwing that inside your XL bag. Pull the clutch out when you're going to lunch and want to give your arm a much-needed rest.

GET IT FOR LESS

If you are trying to save for a much desired designer bag, but the price tag is still out of your budget, check out buying the real thing on eBay or at Tanger Designer Outlet Mall (www.tangeroutlet .com). Tanger—with its extensive inventory of high-quality designer accessories—has locations all over the country. One more special reason I love to shop at Tanger is that this tasteful outlet mall supports various breast cancer and children's charities.

BLOCHBUSTER TIP

A fabric or straw bag is often more appropriate for the summer season than a heavy leather one. The good news is purses in these materials also cost a lot less!

RENT IT

There are companies that actually rent purses! It's a great gimmick. (You can tote a hot Balenciaga Arena bag to your high school reunion for a small fraction of the cost.) But is it really worthwhile? After all, so many others before you have rented the same bag and carried their troubles around in it—do you really want to absorb their bag feng shui? I can understand wanting to put forth the best image possible (that's what I help people do every day). But if you rent a Chanel quilted leather handbag for the big dinner with the bosses, they might not think you really need that raise after all. It can seem fun to rent a bag and suddenly have all the designers at your doorstep, but do you really need to spend the money when it's going to have to eventually go back? If it will lift you out of your doldrums, then knock yourself out. But for $50, I'd rather see you buy a bag inspired by the original on the street.

You have reached the shopping expert finish line. You know your way around department stores, boutiques, websites, and anywhere else you can shop. You'll sweet talk a salesperson to find out about sales early, but you aren't swayed by phony offers. You've brought your shoe and bag fever down a few degrees with my inside information on how to detect quality and reject costly gimmicks. Basically you know it all. But the big question is how to stick to *The Shopping Diet*. How do you keep up your resolve not to fall back into sloppy shopping habits once you close this book? Have no fear of getting fat on lame fashion choices. The prescription for a beautiful and debt-free future is waiting for you in the next and last step.

Step Ten:

Make *The Diet* a Way of Life

In order to be all the shopper you can be, it's time to put down the credit cards and explore what else life has to offer. That's right—if you love something, set it free. The vicious cycle of shopping and returning can no longer be the only activity you do during your spare time. Now that you and your wallet are on *The Shopping Diet,* you have to find other ways to enjoy yourself. Why not start by taking an entire weekend and vowing to stay out of the stores? The point is to make a conscious decision that shopping and spending are no longer a must-have part of your weekend (or weekly) activities. Obviously, your life requires you to shop sometimes. But it will be a welcome change of pace to switch things up and get out of the stores if they've just been serving as a pit stop between breakfast, lunch, dinner . . . and debt. You'll get an extra thrill when you do go to the stores because it won't be the same old merchandise you've already bought out of boredom or put back a hundred times. By this point, you must realize that you've already wasted too much of your life and your salary shopping in excess.

Don't Transfer the Compulsion

My friend swore off buying new clothing for three months. But a funny thing happened on her way to the mall. She became a Crate & Barrel junkie, purchasing three lamps and two new couches to redecorate her perfectly decorated apartment. Don't transfer your fashion shopping compulsion onto other goods. Just because you're not buying sweaters anymore (you have ten good ones in your own personal closet boutique) doesn't mean it's time to buy a third set of dishes or new cutlery that you don't need!

Shopping is shopping and excess is excess, and that includes buying for your home, your kids, or even your friends or family. *The Diet's* rules should be applied to anything that spurs you to spend excessively. Keep strict parameters on the way that you shop for everything. Do you really need those 600-thread-count sheets when 300-count would be comfy enough? Please don't think that just because you're taking control of your shoe habit that it now means you can go to Target and transfer the spending into buying new towels (even if they are affordable) when the ones at home are in perfectly good condition.

The bills for these items will make you feel exactly the same way those clothing bills did at the end of the month— stressed and depressed. Just because you're out of the house and in the vicinity of a store doesn't mean you have to single-handedly stimulate the economy. You don't need another lipstick, vase, nail polish, or gossip magazine. (Turn on E! or TMZ if you're already paying for cable or go online and check out PerezHilton.com or DListed.com if you're already paying for Internet!) When your hands are itching for bags to hold as you walk home, stop and remember, *I'm on The Shopping Diet!* Step up your self-control and stay out of the stores—any stores. Yes, that includes the automotive store, the plant store, and the bakery. You have plenty of better things to do besides shop.

What to Do Besides Shop

It's a big world out there with lots of activities to explore. You must curb your urge to splurge and fill up your time with more worthwhile pursuits. The first step is to stay out of the stores. If you're not in the mall or a shop, then you won't be tempted to buy things that you don't need or duplicate what's already hanging in your closet. At this stage of *The Shopping Diet,* you've become more organized. You've made lists of what you need to purchase. You're condensing and focusing your shopping trips. I'd hate to see you slip and go to the mall on a mission to buy only socks . . . which leads to shoes . . . which leads to a sale . . . and we know how that will end. Start by taking small steps. Break it down. Don't go to the malls or other shops for one weekend. That's easy.

So what can you do to fill your time? Begin to think about all those things you've been meaning to do—from gardening, to helping out at a homeless shelter, to finally organizing all of those photos you took last summer. Take your children to the park, drive to a gorgeous destination, and bask in its natural (and free!) beauty. Carve out romantic time to pamper your partner. Get together that scrapbook you've been wanting to start or call your aunt, who meant so much to you as a child but who you haven't spoken to in months (use Skype—it's free). Or start a blog and tell the world what you're thinking. Take a bike ride to a new destination with Lionel Richie or Beyoncé . . . that's what your iPod's for. Most cities constantly have new art expositions or free concerts going on. Use your newfound time for checking local papers and online for free cultural events in your area. Go outside and smell the roses. I'm being serious. Literally go and tend to your garden and then flop in a lawn chair with a glass of iced tea and just relax for a moment. After all, you deserve it. Now that you've gotten your shopping disorder in order and you have proven to yourself that you are an empowered person who can conquer what you put your mind to, you deserve more than iced tea. You deserve champagne! There isn't that massive stress and clutter in your head that was making you so afraid to be alone. Now it has become calming to take time for you, so go with the flow and just be with you.

The point is to cultivate or initiate other interests in your life that will further stimulate you. Activity begets activity. Starting one thing will create a chain reaction. Doing wonderful new things and meeting new people will help you grow as a person. You can be your own worst enemy or you can be your very best ally. It's your choice now. It may feel familiar and comfortable to fall back into your routine and do what you used to do. But that's a trap. You must alter your perspective. Be the impetus to your own change, resurgence, and growth. Some people are naturally inquisitive and constantly find new and intriguing things to do with their time. Some simply enjoy carving out time for themselves. And others are constantly enrolled and participating in groups and clubs or are surrounded by friends and festivities. You can find new directions and still be true to your own nature. It's as simple as reading a good book or going to visit an old friend. Take a class that you've always thought about trying in order to expand your horizons. You will learn something new to inspire you to make a better change in your life.

Now that wandering the mall is no longer second nature, sleep in on Saturday, take a long walk with your significant other, or cook that great recipe you clipped out six months ago but never tried. I don't care if you even decide to curl up on your couch and take a nap. Just give the stores a rest, and the result will be life-changing on many levels. You'll be saving money and surprising yourself.

SHOPPING ALTERNATIVES

* Take a class: cooking, foreign language, a new instrument, pottery, or even sewing (it will increase your clothing transformation skills).

* Make handmade gifts: Candles, soap, or hand-knits are great for birthdays and holidays (the more you make yourself, the more you save yourself).

✳ Start a side business (you've always made the best brownies at the bake sale or your sewing skills have always been superb—turn your talents into a little extra cash).

✳ Exercise: power walking, running, biking, or another sport you can do on your own.

✳ Play team sports: baseball, hockey, soccer, and so on (you'll not only have fun but will also find other people whose interests are more varied than just shopping).

✳ Try arts and crafts: Let your inner artist flourish!

✳ Get political: Become an active part in the change for you and your community (one small idea can develop into a global shift).

✳ Be a mentor to a child in need.

✳ Volunteer at a local nursing home or hospital.

✳ Go on an ultra-wellness or cleansing diet.

✳ Make your children's lunch, as well as your own, and make healthy choices.

✳ Take a dance class just for fun (samba, anyone?).

✳ Step out of the work–spend cycle and become time-rich.

Gift Giving

Gifts are an extra expense that we come across all the time. You can end up spending a ton of money on them, but—guess what—you don't have to.

PLAN IN ADVANCE

Be on the lookout all year long for inexpensive ideas and presents—and if you see some things at an affordable price in April, who says that you can't buy a few of them and use them as stocking stuffers in December? I keep those pre-thought-of gifts in boxes labeled and categorized for quick easy shopping in my home boutique. Last year, I went into a store where they had a great buy on beautiful little tortoiseshell bowls. Marked down from $40 to $4.99, they were a steal. So I scooped up five of them as potential gifts. Soon these pretty bowls were wrapped in gorgeous paper with perfect bows. I sent them out and didn't feel a qualm about not spending a lot of money. A very close business associate of mine tells me to this day that she loves that bowl and keeps it on her desk as a business card holder. *The perceived value of a gift is not directly correlated with its actual price.*

The high economical and emotional cost of gifts comes from shopping in a hurry. It's not just the money that you're spending on a gift, but it's the amount of time and stress that becomes an additional price. Let's say it's your friend's birthday and you spend all week worrying about what to get her, but by the evening of the party you still haven't found the perfect item. So what do you do? You frantically run to the store and get an overpriced bottle of champagne. You spent an entire week stressing (waste of time) and more than $100 on a gift that isn't that meaningful (waste of money). The bottom line is: When it comes to gifts, avoid procrastination.

The same idea applies to gifts for children. If they're in grade school, the kiddie birthday parties are happening every week. You are expected to bring a gift to every party. It's about being prepared and buying in bulk. I'm not saying to buy the same thing, but there's nothing wrong with going to Target or Costco, and if you find a cute knapsack, buying it in a few different colors. Be prepared—it saves money, time, and stress.

REGIFTING

Though many people feel that regifting is tacky, I like to think of the process as the gift that keeps on giving. Let's say a friend gave you Gucci sunglasses for your birthday. While you appreciated the thoughtfulness behind the gift, you don't actually need those sunglasses (you've got ten other pairs), but you have another friend who loves all things Gucci. These sunglasses could be regifted as the second friend's Christmas present. It will save you money and time because you don't have to return the Gucci glasses or look for a Christmas present for your friend. Regifting is often better than returning a gift, especially one without a receipt, where you'll end up getting $5 instead of the original price of $50 because the item is now sitting in the sales section.

In my home, I have made my own regifting station. It's easy to do. Reserve several bins or large baskets for house presents that you have received but know you won't use. (You can also use the bins for items that you have picked up on sale to give later on.) To make life easier, categorize the containers by group (men's, women's, kids, etc.). Near these bins in an accessible place, store your gift wrapping, gift bags, tape, tags, bows, and cards. This way, the gifts will be ready at a moment's notice.

WHEN IN DOUBT, GIVE MONEY

If you don't want to get caught up in asking friends what they want or need for their next birthday, a simple, easy, and much-appreciated solution is the prepaid gift card. One of my best friends has moved three times within the past four years and has two small children and an employment-challenged husband. I couldn't even begin to know what they need because they need a lot—and only they can understand their priorities. Last year for the holidays, I sent four $50 gift cards, which allowed each person in the family to get his or her own little necessities or make one big purchase for the entire family. The choice was theirs and it was greatly appreciated. Now more than ever, it's easy to give gift cards. Literally all retailers have their own, from iTunes to Pottery Barn to Burger King. So if you're worried that gift cards are too impersonal, make it personal by buying your gift card at a store you know your friend or family member loves. You can even buy these cards online and have them delivered right to the person's door—now, what's more personal than that?

JUST SAY NO

Your friends might be having a big wedding or birthday bash. But if you are seriously strapped for cash, it's okay to say no. No excuses, no lies. Just the truth. You're sorry, but you can't afford to attend the event with a gift. You can offer to help with the event in some way or send a beautiful note later. Use your skills instead of spending cash. You can even take the host to lunch once you have the money (and time) to afford it. The best gift is your presence.

TAKING IT ON THE ROAD

Destination events are incredibly costly—suddenly you're required to buy plane tickets, a hotel room, transportation, and more on top of a gift (and probably an outfit). If your wallet just can't go the extra distance, it's okay to ask the hosts straight up: "I can either come to your wedding or I can buy you a great gift. You choose!" I guarantee that they will choose your presence over the present if they are really your friends.

Guilt Offerings

Now that you've learned to save and eliminate excessive spending, please don't waste that hard-earned cash by loaning it to family or friends. You shouldn't be their personal ATM (even if your teenage son knows how to push your buttons with a PIN that never fails). You can end up paying for other people's shopping binges because you're a parent, a sister, or just a nice person. You simply can't afford to consume cash calories for another person when you're on *The Shopping Diet*. It's enough to make sure that you don't exceed your own caloric intake each day.

Yes, I know that family and friends have a great way of making you feel guilty if you don't open your wallet and act generously. But, from here on out, I want you to think of emotional spending as the equivalent of arriving at a blazing fire and tossing a basket of cash into the flames. You're feeding the fire and making bad habits burn even brighter. This is often the case when it comes to paying the tab for loved ones. Yes, you can throw money on the problem right away, but in most cases it won't help them in the big picture. And it certainly won't help you.

Food for Thought

* Are you spending money just to keep the peace with friends and family?
* Are you giving away money to help others when you don't have enough to help yourself?
* Does everyone always come to you for a loan?

* When you're out with certain people, does the bill always magically float to you?
* Do you choose to eat in expensive restaurants, which you really can't afford, because you want to impress others or because you're too afraid or embarrassed to tell them otherwise?
* Do you grab your friends' purchases at a store and say, "I'll get this"?
* Do you cosign for loans on big-ticket items such as cars and houses, even when the purchase has nothing to do with you and could put your own good credit score at risk?
* On the rare times you find yourself with extra cash (is there such thing?), do you end up giving it to friends or relatives so that they can lead a better life?

If you answered yes to any of these questions, you are participating in emotional spending, which often translates into emotional blackmail. It's time to get control over your feelings, your money, and your relationships. If you can't control what is yours, who will? Make loans with the same new purpose you now bring to shopping trips.

What If You Slip Up?

Please don't punish yourself with guilt. You just immediately get back on *The Shopping Diet*. One binge doesn't break this diet. It simply bends it a bit. No one is perfect, and the key to long-term success is finding the power to stop, regroup, and get back on your plan after any misstep. Here are a few mantras to keep in mind *before* you are tempted to go hog wild with your AmEx.

* You're in control of your own destiny and this includes your happiness. It's so tough to be happy when you're worried about bills.
* You can't get a good night's sleep if you're counting your credit card bills instead of sheep.
* You don't want to live like an addict (no matter how in control you seem to others) who covets the thrill of the moment without thinking about the consequences.
* You're an interesting person who has more to explore in life than the shoe department at Saks.
* Your closet is so clean and organized now—don't do anything that'll mess it up!
* You really don't need extra things, but you can always find an important use for more of your money.

BLOCH**BUSTER** TIP

If you find yourself on a shopping binge, don't freak—just get back on the plan. Keep your receipts, take the stuff back, put that money in your savings account, and don't feel guilty. Guilt is part of the reason you overspent in the first place.

Your Financial Health Checkup

Remember your Diet Log, that list of spending versus earning you completed? Just because you do the list once doesn't mean you shouldn't revisit it periodically. Certainly any sort of major life event (including marriage, divorce, relocation, a new job, or a job layoff) means that you should revisit your finances. There's no shame in taking it all down a notch when it comes to spending. It's not sad that you can't shell out as much money on nonessentials. You're just playing it closer to the vest while you look for new financial opportunities. Again, don't feel like you're the most denied person in the world. Feel lucky that you are in control of your destiny.

A FRIENDLY REMINDER

When you need a reminder of why you aren't at the mall buying the latest and greatest things, take a look at your credit card balance. It's actually going down! The only thing you should be buying now is buying back your good credit and peace of mind. Think of paying off your bills and the calmness that will be achieved at your next purchase. You're now able to pay off more each month. Since your debt is lessening, so is your minimum payment.

Do yourself a favor—just paying the minimum on any credit card debt will not actually get you out of debt. The banks have set up a system to keep you beholden to them and owing them for life. When you're paying the minimum, you're only paying off the interest. Your principle will remain the same. Even if you start paying an additional $20 or $50 over the minimum due, you will be paying off at least some of the principle. It will then, in turn, bring the amount of interest down and subsequently your total payments will decrease as well. And don't go on a spending spree when you see your diminished credit card balance. There is no reward in using your extra cash to go shopping. That's the one step forward and two steps back syndrome rearing its ugly head. Trust me—there is no better feeling than taking a high balance and watching it zoom down to the zero mark!

A terrific way to make sure your crystal glass (or paper cup) is always half full—no matter what curves life throws you—is to follow the Triple-Pay Plan. It's simple. Whenever money comes in or has been saved somewhere else in your life, divide it into three so that you can pay for your past, present, and future. Part of the money goes toward your past debt. Part of it should go toward the present expenses, and part of it should be saved for what you need (or don't even know you want) in the future. You can't accomplish the Triple-Pay Plan with constant unconscious shopping and spending. You must focus on finding ways to cut back and save on your day-to-day expenses. The Plan is a great way to relieve yesterday's debt, make today easier, and keep you looking forward to tomorrow.

Let's say you quit smoking. A pack of cigarettes costs roughly $10, and you were buying seven packs a week. That's $70 a week and approximately $300 a month spent on tobacco! Now that you have broken the bad habit, you can use that extra $300 (or $3,600 over a year) and apply it to the Triple-Pay Plan. Divide this savings by three and put one-third toward past debt, one-third toward current expenses, and one-third toward something you need in the future that you haven't been able to afford. At the end of one year, you could pay off an extra $1,200 of accumulated debt (which will in turn bring your interest levels down and garner even more savings). You could also have put an additional $100 every month toward your cell phone bill. And you've still got $1,200 for something special in the future that you couldn't otherwise afford—perhaps a great weekend vacation. You can apply this plan to many aspects of your life—think about all the things you can cut back on (bring lunch to work instead of buying it; make coffee at home instead of buying those expensive lattes; cut back on your premium cable channels). And don't be too lazy or embarrassed to use coupons, coupons, coupons—they are there for the sole purpose of saving you money, so use them! I love Feedthepig .com, which offers endless (and free) solutions on how to find savings for any lifestyle.

Closet Maintenance Plan

Part of sticking to *The Shopping Diet* will include bi-yearly exams of your closet. I suggest making your assessments at the beginning of the spring and fall seasons. Once a year, you should even take your clothing out again and place it in piles—keepers, fixers, donations, giveaways. You know the drill. This is crucial to not letting your spending habits slip. Now that you've gotten your addiction under control, this maintenance will be so much faster and will also be a great way for you to appreciate your progress. I recommend making that date with yourself early in the year by marking it on your calendar.

Part of this process is keeping a special place, such as a box or a bin, for all of the clothing that needs fixing or upkeep. On the same day that you evaluate your closet, you will deal with the fixer bin. The point is that you have a regular seasonal appointment with that bin and your closet in order to keep things clean and prevent a mess from building up. Recognize that you have changed your life in a major way. Take excellent care of your closet, which you have worked so hard for. It will make everything else in your life feel that much better.

Celebration Time

Congratulations! You're in control of your shopping and spending now more than you've ever been. By taking the steps to transform the way you think, shop, and spend your money, you've achieved a huge accomplishment. I hope that you're feeling as powerful as you are. We all have physical and emotional piles of stuff that create chaos and disorder in our lives. You have chosen to walk out of this trap and into a beautiful life on your terms.

What's even more important is realizing that life's real rewards don't have a price tag on them or reside with all of the mediocre shirts in the middle of a store. Your joy doesn't always come in a box that says Prada or Chanel. Your true rewards come from gifts in life that do not cost a thing. That includes friendship, family, and the joy of having a stress-free

and productive life. *The Shopping Diet* is not about depriva-
tion; it's about controlled spending and the occasional extrav-
agance when you have done the responsible things first.
When you understand your impulses, you are under less pressure to act upon them and can make more room to bring joy
to yourself as well as to those around you.

I will ask you one more thing. Every day, consider what
you have done. Consider the steps you have taken to get your
life back in control by controlling your negative shopping
habits. Every day, reexamine how you once shopped in an uncomfortable, expensive frenzy and be thankful it is not that
way now. Every day, remember that good clean feeling of con-
structing a well-organized wardrobe. Read over the steps
whenever you need a refresher. Feel the freedom to shop responsibly for what you need. Life is not pain-free. But remember, we learn from our discontent, and then we have that
choice to change. Be grateful for all of the abundance you
have been given.

Now, take a look at your new closet, then look in the
mirror and repeat after me:

> I have the incentive and the desire to make and main-
> tain my own happiness.

> I have the choice to never get into that all-consuming
> shopping and spending rut again.

> I put value in the better things in life, and I don't have
> to go to the mall to find them.

I have always had, and will continue to have, a free ticket to the boutique of positive thinking, well-being, and simple abundance, as well as the peace of mind that accompanies a brand-new attitude and a brand-new closet.

The Shopping Diet Directory

I've listed below some websites, stores, and charities you might want to check out. The directory and the details provided about them is based on information collected while I was writing this book in May 2010, but the specifics might change over time. So be sure to review sales and any other relevant terms when you visit the sites. Enjoy your smart shopping! XO, Phillip

Sample Sale Announcement Websites

DailyCandy - *www.dailycandy.com*
Probably one of the most well-known sites offering an insider's guide to what's new, hot, and undiscovered in most major cities across the USA (including New York, Los Angeles, Chicago, Boston, Washington D.C., Miami, Atlanta, Dallas, Philadelphia, Seattle, and San Francisco) as well as across the globe and the World Wide Web. DailyCandy's free daily email newsletter notifies subscribers about upcoming entertainment events, store openings, travel ideas, and, most important, sample sales! If you sign up for the site's daily tips advisories you will always be in the know. The site gives you insider tips tailored to your city.

Fashion Week Daily - *www.dailyfrontrow.com*
Fashion Week Daily, known online as Daily Front Row, gives you constant updates on fashion events, news, and trends all in one

user-friendly and informative space. The site gives users a look into the goings-on of the "fashion elite," including photos, party coverage, press launches, and sample-sale alerts. Sign up for the daily email blast to learn about key sales happening both online and in fashion city centers.

Lazar - *www.lazarshopping.com*

The first of its kind, Lazar Shopping began publishing in 1986 to inform bargain hunters of unadvertised designer sales. A subscription to the site provides a complete guide to sample sales in New York City, including locations, dates, payment methods, and a description of what you'll find. Many sample sales will only advertise with Lazar, making its list all the more comprehensive. The site features a free list of highlighted New York City sample sales. Subscribers also get daily email alerts for upcoming sales as well as links to Lazar's "Tip Of The Day" and "Designer Profiles."

New York Magazine - *www.nymag.com*

Includes a sales calendar for the week along with best bets, features such as "Fashion For Under $100," trend reports, popular store listings, and boutique openings.

Time Out magazine - *www.timeout.com*

Offers a good but short list of sample sales for the current week as well as boutique openings and sales.

Sample Sale Websites

Beyond the Rack - *www.beyondtherack.com*

Beyond the Rack, is the new, up and coming sample-sale site that everyone is talking about. Even Khloe Kardashian was all up in tweets about it! This site is by invite only, yet has an option to allow the site viewer to join its waiting list. Sample-sale sites' exclusivity might be frustrating so don't get your La Perla panties in a twist. Once you have access to these deals they will knock your designer shoes off. With featured designers such as Gucci, Roberto Cavalli,

Marc Jacobs, D&G, Versace, Fendi, and Armani, I know I wouldn't want everyone having access to these great steals! So, find a friend who's a part of it or get on the waiting list so you can get beyond the rack!

Editors' Closet - *www.editorscloset.com*

Editors' Closet organizes online confidential sample sales on high-end products from prestigious brands, including designer apparel, accessories, electronics, jewelry, and children's products, all backed by warranties. Membership to this site is free, although you do need to be referred by a friend or sign up on a waiting list to join the select club. You will receive an email invitation notifying you of an upcoming sale 48 hours before it begins. Retail prices are generally reduced by 30% to 75%.

Gilt Groupe - *www.gilt.com*

INVITE ONLY. Gilt Groupe provides access, by invitation only, to women's, men's, and children's coveted designer fashion and luxury brands, including Marc Jacobs, Hervé Léger, Christian Louboutin, and many more, at prices of up to 70% off retail. Each sale lasts 36 hours and features hand selected styles from a single designer. Members are sent email notifications 24 hours before a sale goes live.

HauteLook - *www.hautelook.com*

HauteLook is another members-only club that organizes time-limited sales on designer brands. Usually these sales offer discounts of 50% to 75% off of retail prices. The site is free to join and does not require an invitation from an existing member. HauteLook sends its members a daily email listing the sales that will be opening and closing on its website that day. The site offers products across the board, including designer apparel, high-end beauty products, and even brand name furniture and housewares.

Ideeli - *www.ideeli.com*

Membership to the "Second Row" club on this website is free and easy. However, to gain access to more exclusive sales and to shop sales an hour in advance of their official launch, Ideeli will upgrade you to a "First Row" membership for $6.99 USD per month. Apart from its designer sample sales, the site also offers giveaways and promotions to members.

Billion Dollar Babes - *www.billiondollarbabes.com*

Perhaps one of the most well known sample sale sites on the internet, Billion Dollar Babes was created in 2001 to showcase discounted products from top designers. The company actually came up with the concept of the multi-designer sample sale and has hosted numerous sample sale events in cities across the USA, including Los Angeles, New York, Chicago, and beyond. These sales are not only great shopping opportunities, they're also a ton of fun, complete with cocktails, beauty bars, and swag bags. And the company has now taken those infamous sales to the Web! Participating designers have included Dolce & Gabbana, Valentino, Diane Von Furstenberg, Chloé, Catherine Malandrino, and more. Billion Dollar Babes holds three high-end designer sales per week online, each one lasting 48 hours, with discounts of up to 80%. Initial membership is free; however, you can choose to upgrade in order to receive advance notice of sales and be able to shop them earlier for a yearly fee.

Rue La La - *www.ruelala.com*

INVITE ONLY. Rue La La is an exclusive online destination where members can shop premier brand, private sale boutiques, each open for just a brief period of time. The site focuses on offering a well-edited selection of merchandise from the best brand names in the world. If you invite someone to join the club, you receive an additional $10 off your next purchase. Membership is invite-only and an existing member has to sponsor you. You can also put your name forward without a member's sponsorship to be considered if and when the site has room for new members.

Shopstyle.com™ - *www.shopstyle.com*

ShopStyle is a social shopping destination that brings together the most on-trend brands and boutiques. This site allows users to cross-shop hundreds of thousands of online outlets to find the best product at the best price. The community pages combine fashion and design trends with tools to allow users to interpret the latest styles. You can also create, share, and shop personalized looks.

Off-Price Websites

Avelle, The New Bag Borrow or Steal - *www.bagborroworsteal.com*

The concept of this revolutionary site is simple, why buy when you can borrow. Not only will you be saving tons of money by becoming a member but it's also a greener way to "shop." Instead of paying $1200 for one bag, for a very low monthly fee you can have access to thousands of authentic, designer bags, jewelry, sunglasses, and watches. You can rent by the week, month, or season. Bag Borrow or Steal makes it easy to dress to impress without breaking the bank. When you're ready for a new look, just send back what you have, shipping is free!

Shopzilla - *www.shopzilla.com*

With Shopzilla, you no longer have to search through hundreds of sites to find the best deal on that pair of True Religion jeans you have been coveting. You can just enter the item you are looking for into their search bar and the results, including price, store, and item description will be nicely displayed so you can easily scroll through to find who has the best deal. You can literally search millions of products, 80 million to be exact, to find anything from patio furniture to Chanel sunglasses.

Bluefly - *www.bluefly.com*

Bluefly is probably one of the best known off-price web-exclusive retailers in the world. It is known for its wide selection of discount designer clothing for men and women. The site also makes shopping a dream, organizing product by occasion, color, designer, bestsellers, or style. Be sure to search their Clearance/Sale page for even lower bargains. This site is also great for discounted designer evening-wear and unique shoe finds.

eBay - *www.ebay.com*

eBay truly does live up to its name as "The World's Marketplace." It enables trade on a local, national, and international basis where literally millions of items are traded each day. eBay is a great resource for the fashion savvy as it is usually the place to locate the hard-to-find sold-out "It" items at lesser prices. Also be sure to look to eBay for vintage clothes, jewelry, and accessories at a fraction of the retail price. Shoes are also easy to find as the site allows you to search by size, color, and designer.

Overstock.com® - *www.overstock.com*

This is a fantastic online outlet that sells off liquidated and excess stock including designer and name brand goods. It offers products from apparel to furniture to electronics to toys. This is, essentially, one of the Internet's biggest outlet malls. If you join Club O and shop regularly, shipping is free and you can take advantage of further discounts on items for sale. Membership costs $19.95 USD/year and allows you access to a further discount of 5% on most items as well as access to coupons and promotions.

Designer Websites With Good Sales

Calypso - *www.calypso-celle.com*

Known for their fashionable and effortless resort wear, Calypso carries upscale clothing by a variety of smaller designers. Their signature silhouettes are designed to transcend seasons and accommodate a woman's ever evolving lifestyle. Whether you are in the early stages of your pregnancy or experiencing a little fluctuation in weight, the incredibly versatile and chic designs at Calypso will flatter your figure and ensure that you look sophisticated and stylish. They have a number of clothing stores across the country as well as Paris and St. Barth and a few specialty home stores in California and New York. A few times a year they have mega sales, both online and in stores, where you can score amazing pieces for a fraction of the price.

Chickdowntown - *www.chickdowntown.com*

This Pittsburgh-based boutique specializes in bold, statement-making dresses. Sales are ongoing, allowing you to swipe up Missoni tank dresses and Biba caftans for half their original prices. Now that's a bargain.

Endless Shoes and More . . . - *www.endless.com*

Endless.com always has major sales on designer shoes, including Givenchy, Giuseppe Zanotti, Roberto Cavalli, and Stuart Weitzman—many with 80% discounts. The site is a fantastic resource for the accessory-minded shopper and offers free overnight shipping, free return shipping, and a 365-day returns window. With the option to choose size, color, designer, and even price range, it gives the shopper who likes endless possibilities a no hassle online shopping experience.

Intermix - *www.intermixonline.com*

The website for the popular boutique chain, Intermix, offers the same renowned mix of established and emerging designers. The site offers a "High/Low" range of items from moderate to designer in unexpected combinations. Expect to find key items from labels like Stella McCartney, Hervé Léger, JBrand, Sass & Bide, Chloé, LaRok, and Diane Von Furstenberg. The site also features easy-to-use trend reports, editorials, and new designer profiles. Sales offer these well-known designer labels at a fraction of the price, usually discounted for upwards of 50% off.

Net-A-Porter - *www.net-a-porter.com*

This is the world's premier online luxury fashion retailer. It offers a comparable and well-edited selection of high end designer women's fashion labels taken right from the runway. The packaging is impeccable—everything arrives at your door in beautiful and sophisticated black boxes with big bows. The site also features fashion editorials, updated weekly with new content and product, much like an online fashion magazine. The sales on this site are legendary and occur on a seasonal basis.

Piperlime - *www.piperlime.gap.com*

Run by Gap Inc, Piperlime is a fantastic go-to site for the shoe addict that sells mid to high end designer labels. The Lime Tag Sale offers up to 50% off an exhaustive assortment of bags and shoes from names like Marc by Marc Jacobs, Kooba, Pucci, and more. Click on Final Sale for the absolute cheapest finds. Another great saving tip is to combine your purchases from Gap, Banana Republic, Old Navy, and Piperlime together for one flat shipping rate. Be sure to keep an eye out for me friend and fellow celebrity stylist, Rachel Zoe, who also has her own section of favorite shoe picks and bestsellers.

REVOLVEClothing - *www.revolveclothing.com*

This site offers the best in women's and men's designer clothing and accessories as well as an eclectic mix of lifestyle goods. You can always find the latest trends and the hottest looks of the season from designers like Catherine Malandrino, Haute Hippie, and Charlotte Ronson here. The site features over 400 brands and offers free worldwide shipping, free returns, and live operator assistance, what's not to love!

On top of having great seasonal deals and a lust worthy sale section, you can also join their members only outlet site reverse-reverse .com where you can enjoy huge savings on past seasons designer wears.

Shopbop - *www.shopbop.com*

This is the go-to site for all things hip, trendy, and fun. It is considered a one-stop shopping destination for women's apparel, shoes, and accessories from such up-and-coming designers as Alexander Wang, Phillip Lim, Geren Ford, and Elizabeth & James. The site also features a fantastic online magazine and trend report, updated weekly. Sales on seasonal items range from 20% to 70% off retail, making it easy for the fashion-forward shopper to find some satisfying bargains.

Vivre - *www.vivre.com*

This website also offers high-end labels and designer exclusives. Eva Jeanbart-Lorenzotti is the driving force behind the multifaceted world of VIVRE. She explains "VIVRE is a journey of discovery—a celebration of artistry, originality, and the incredible harmony of the different cultural and global treasures all around us." A varied mix of indulgences are regularly available at discounts for up to 50% and browsing is made easy as items can be sorted by style, prices, and recent additions. The real prizes on this site, however, are their exclusive items found only online, including jeweled snake bracelets from Roberto Cavalli and Michael Kors' fur-trimmed cardigans.

Zappos - *www.zappos.com*

A great website for finding a huge selection of shoes, clothing, and accessories. They have competitive prices and offer a wide variety of designers so you can find an extensive selection of inexpensive items, designer items, and everything in between. They also have a wonderful return policy so you don't have to worry if the item you purchased isn't quite right, you have 365 days to return it! Now that's what I call customer service.

Outlet Malls

Chelsea Premium Outlets/Woodbury Commons - *www.premiumoutlets.com*

This chain of outlet malls brings together some of the finest luxury brands and offers them at a savings of 25%-65% off retail price. With over 40 outlets across the US and hundreds of designer fashion, shoes, housewares, children's, and accessory brands, including Gucci, BCBG, Fendi, Prada, Chanel, Burberry, Chloé, 7 For All Mankind, Catherine Malandrino, Nine West, and Cole Hahn, Balenciaga, Brioni, Bottega Veneta, Diane Von Furstenberg, Dolce & Gabbana, CH Carolina Herrera, Escada, Emilio Pucci, Elie Tahari, Giorgio Armani, Hugo Boss, John Varvatos, G-Star Raw, La Perla, Lululemon Athletica, M Missoni, Maidenform, MaxMara, Roberto Cavalli, Oscar De La Renta, Ralph Lauren, Rochester Big

& Tall, Ferragamo, Disney Store, Versace, Yves Saint Laurent, Valentino, Zenga, Timberland, Theory, and Thomas Pink this is a perfect destination for any smart shopper looking for legendary brands and bargains. Their website is easy to use, and even lists their phone numbers by designer outlet store so you can inquire about specific must-have items at easy to afford prices; for a stylist that's a must have feature because my clients know exactly what they want! The Chelsea Premium Outlets VIP Shopper Club provides members with periodic email updates on centers, special discounts, a free VIP Coupon Book, and added savings in the VIP Lounge. There is no charge to be a member and you can opt-out at any time.

Prime Outlets - *www.primeoutlets.com*

This outlet chain leads the category in hosting some of the world's most renowned brand names and luxury labels. The portfolio has recently added high-end designer and name brand tenants such as Saks Fifth Avenue OFF 5th, Neiman Marcus Last Call, Giorgio Armani, Barney's New York Outlet, Betsey Johnson, A/X Armani Exchange, Baccarat/Lalique, Burberry, Calvin Klein, Ralph Lauren, Catherine Malandrino, Ed Hardy, Fendi, Hush Puppies, Hartmann Luggage, James Perse, JCREW, Judith Ripka, LL Bean, Hanes, Playtex, Levis, Loro Piana, Max Azria, Michael Kors, Movado, Tori Burch, Calypso, Coach, DKNY, Victoria's Secret Outlet, and more. Prime Outlets has more than 30 locations across the US and offers frequent shoppers a Rewards Program, called the 1Club. The 1Club allows members to enjoy exclusive weekly offers across all brands as well as access to Prime Outlets promotions and events.

Tanger Outlets - *www.tangeroutlet.com*

With over thirty locations across the USA, this outlet chain covers everything from apparel and footwear to linens and housewares across a number of leading brand names and designer labels, including Williams-Sonoma, Harry and David, Le Creuset, Restoration Hardware, Calvin Klein, Barney's New York, Armani, Kate Spade, Hugo Boss, Lane Bryant, Michael Kors, Timberland, Tumi, Stuart Weitzman, Nike, DKNY Donna Karen New York, DKNY Jeans, True Religion, Saks Fifth Avenue OFF 5th, BCBG and what's a great outfit without a little sparkle, you can even afford to get something extra glamourous at Ultra Diamonds. You can save even more during the outlets' centerwide Sidewalk Sales, merchant tent sales, gift with purchase promotions, and other special events. You can also download coupons from the chain's website for even further savings. If you shop frequently, you can become a member of the TangerClub to receive exclusive benefits including Centerwide Coupon Books, a $10 Tanger Gift Card on your birthday, free stroller rental, and special gift and web offers.

Off Price Retailers

Barneys New York - *www.barneys.com*

Style savvy shoppers can find the same type of beautiful clothing and designer brands that line the racks at Barneys New York at a lower price point at Barneys Co-op. It began as a department within Barneys, but due to its popularity grew into a free standing store. Barneys Co-op can now be found in numerous locations nationwide, even numerous outlets shopping centers. The only thing better than designer labels is getting them at discount prices. They often have huge sales that offer up to 70 to 80% off.

Burlington Coat Factory - *www.burlingtoncoatfactory.com*

It's not just for coats anymore! In fact, this off-price retailer now houses a great assortment of current, high-quality designer and name-brand goods at up to 60% less than the leading department store. Apart from men's, women's, and children's apparel, they also feature bedding and home décor in store only. They now offer fabulous sparkle as well, featuring the affordable high quality Ultra Diamonds. There are always tons of discounts available at all store locations to help chop that bargain down even more! And for a smart gift idea, they have great gift cards for any occasion!

Century 21 - *www.c21stores.com*

Century 21 is one of New York fashionista's best kept secrets because it's only available in New York and New Jersey. Department stores have become an icon in the world of off-price retailing in the NYC tri-state area. For the fashion driven bargain shopper this is definitely the place for you! The clothes are high end, commonly European fashions that carry very chic avant garde apparel. With designers such as Betsy Johnson, D&G, Stella McCartney, and Givenchy, it's for people with high end taste but a reasonable budget in mind. The stores carry everything from cosmetics, accessories, men's and women's apparel, children's products, shoes, housewares, and home furnishings at 40 to 70% off regular retail prices. Even though the locations are limited, this has come to be known by fashionistas world wide as a must shop destination.

Daffy's - www.daffys.com
With 18 stores in New York, New Jersey, and Pennsylvania, Daffy's offers designer labels at impressively low prices. Stocking high quality, recognizable labels at a fraction of the price, the chain has become a destination for smart shoppers. Membership to Daffy's Club is free and will give you access to new arrival announcements, promotions, and trend reports.

DSW - www.dsw.com
DSW (Designer Show Warehouse) is a shoe shopping destination for style-conscious men and women who are looking for great buys. I often shop there for my family members and my clients. Inventory is ever-changing and labels range from high end like Stuart Weitzman and Gucci to Jessica Simpson, Nine West, and Steve Madden. DSW is also a great place to purchase basic shoes like sneakers and boots at fantastic prices. Outlets are located across the country. If you are a frequent shopper, join the DSW Rewards Program. Membership is free and you receive reward certificates for every 1500 points earned as well as birthday gift certificates and special online offers. Each year, the store also offers two double-points shopping days for its members as well as advance notice on all sales, clearance, and upcoming opportunities for bonus points.

Filene's Basement - *www.filenesbasement.com*

Filene's Basement is the go-to destination for rare and deeply discounted designer finds. This off-price retailer created the Automatic Mark Down System which states that the longer an item remains unsold, the more the price will be reduced (first 25%, then 50%, then 75%). The chain sports locations across the country and offers an impressive selection of European and American designers. Filene's buys close-out stock from many of the country's most high-end retailers and offers it at a fraction of the price. Although the store itself can seem a little overwhelming and it may take you a whole afternoon to find your treasure, it's well worth it! Be sure to always check the mark down racks, where items are offered at up to 90% off the retail price. And always make a point to visit The Vault, where you can find the most upscale designer labels. The store also offers Filene's Fan Club, a rewards program offered to frequent shoppers. There is no card or points to earn. Instead, members receive 15% off for one shopping day in the spring and fall as well as a 15% birthday discount and special email alerts giving them advance notice of special events, new arrivals, and other great Basement deals.

Loehmann's - *www.loehmanns.com*

Perhaps one of the most well-known off-price specialty designer retailers in the US, Loehmann's offers couture and designer fashions, current in-season merchandise, and frequent new arrivals all at prices 30% to 65% less than the leading department store. With more than 65 stores in 16 states, the store features such top fashion labels as Diane Von Furstenberg, Dolce & Gabbana, Marc Jacobs, Donna Karan, Michael Kors, and more. The chain also has an Insider Club for their customers, which gives members additional savings with a points program and birthday discounts, plus advance notice of sales and new designer arrival updates. I've often used Loehmann's as my go to resource when doing makeovers on a budget for daytime television shows.

Marshall's and TJMaxx – The TJX Group - *www.marshallsonline.com* and *www.tjmaxx.com*

This chain always makes for a great treasure hunt shopping experience. With off-price labels in both fashion and housewares, stock changes on a daily basis so make sure to check in periodically for great buys. There are more than 2500 locations across the US, making the chain the biggest and boldest member of the off-price retailing family. The store also offers customers a fantastic Rewards Program. With the TJX Rewards Card, you can earn points on every purchase you make at TJ Maxx or its partner chains like Marshall's, HomeGoods, and AJ Wright. Spend as little as $200 and you will automatically receive a $10 TJX Rewards Certificate to put towards your next purchase. There is also no annual fee and you receive 10% off your first in-store purchase with the card.

Neiman Marcus Last Call Clearance Centers - *www.nmlastcallstore.com*

All overstock and off-season merchandise from both Neiman Marcus and Bergdorf Goodman stores come to these outlet centers and are given even further discounts. Check the clearance centers website periodically to take note of up-and-coming events, like Buy More Save More Clearances which allows customers to receive further discounts when they buy three or more selected items. And if you open a Neiman's credit card, you will save an additional 5% off your entire purchase.

Nordstrom Rack - *www.shop.nordstrom .com/c/6016611/0~2377475~601611*

Nordstrom Rack carries merchandise from Nordstrom stores and Nordstrom.com at 50 to 60% off original Nordstrom prices. You will also find a wide selection of brand name apparel, accessores, and shoes purchased specially for Nordstrom Rack at a savings of 30 to 70% off. New merchandise arrives daily and one of my favorite things about Nordstrom's rack because my clients and friends come in all shapes and sizes, they even have a variety of petite/plus sizes available.

Payless Shoesource - *www.payless.com*
There are nearly 4600 locations of this retail chain, making them easy to locate and easy to shop. Look for such well-known brands as Airwalk, American Eagle, Champion, and Disney. They have taken their bargain fashion shoes to the next level with Sex and The City designer and fashionable friend and icon Patricia Field's sexy shoe line. In addition, my boy, innovative and cutting edge designer Christian Siriano has created a trendy contemporary line that has both sexy, casual, and business versatility. Their styles are standardized across the country, so they offer a quick and easy solution for last minute shoe emergencies. With dyeables always in stock, you can always match your shoes to your fantastic outfit! Yet, best of all, frequent shoppers are also able to take advantage of special sales, including Buy 1, Get 1 Free or Buy 1 Get 1 Half Off.

Ross Dress For Less - *www.rossdressforless.com*
Expect to find designer and brand name fashions for women, men, children, and home at savings of up to 20% to 60% compared to department and specialty stores. They are equipped with fashion buyers who scope NYC and LA market who work closely with manufactures to get the consumer the best deal possible! They are all about the bargain hunter and helping you get the best deal possible.

Fast Yet Fashionable

American Apparel - *www.americanapparel.net*
When looking for very cool, hip, and sexy pieces with solid quality, this is the place. The leading brand when it comes to affordable basics for men, women, and children. This is the place for the perfect cotton T-shirt or stretch miniskirt. My personal favorite are the ultra sheer tees that come in oodles of colors, they are my summer must have go to for looking sexy, yet smart. They hit the nail on the head when it comes to trends they capture fashion basics at the best, all styles are available in a wide range of colors. With stores throughout the United States and a strong accessible website, it is a great fast fashion solution. Better still, everything is proudly made in the USA.

American Eagle Outfitters - *www.ae.com*

This trendy hotspot tends to cater to a younger crowd, but it's a great place to go for all American classics like cotton tanks and madras button downs. The clothing has a girl next door meets beach chick feel, think ruffly tops paired with worn in cutoffs. You can find must have boyfriend separates here, so you no longer have to steal your man's comfy jeans and baggy shirts. Don't forget to check out their versatile camisoles, swimwear, and accessories while you're there. AE is definitely a great pick for stylish guys and gals and young hot celebrities like Tailor Swift too!

Anthropologie - *www.anthropologie.com*

Owned by Urban Outfitters, Anthropologie offers a gorgeous variety of vintage inspired bohemian chic and special pieces so your every-day office wear is not just *everyday,* they offer clothing, accessories, housewares, body care, and furniture to give every area of your life an extra boost of personal style. Even though it's a chain, Anthropologie does a great job at making you feel like you are discovering one-of-a-kind treasures at the world's best vintage shop, but at realistic prices. Their sales are a must, with tons of variety the odds are low you won't find something to suite your voracious appetite. If you can't make it to one of their shops, their website is great too. It often carries styles you can't find at the brick and mortar stores and it has a great styling tool to help you put together outfits. It's like having your own stylist right in your computer.

Bebe - *www.bebe.com*

Bebe carries a variety of contemporary women's apparel and acces-sories. Their clothing is flirty and fun and tends to be on the sexier side. Bebe aspires to cater to stylish women who aren't afraid to show off their curves. They have recently teamed up with the E! TV's sexy reality stars the Kardashian sisters to put out a collection of fun, feminine, form-fitting pieces at functional affordable prices.

Club Monaco - *www.clubmonaco.com*

A great place to find classic men's and women's clothing with a con-temporary twist, they have all the basic shapes like trenches, pencil skirts, shift dresses and jeans but made with modern tailoring and fashion-forward fabrics. If their well fitted men's suits and figure flattering women's pants don't draw you right in, they also have great incentives that are sure to make you a loyal shopper. They offer flexible hours for busy shoppers, private after-hour shopping parties for you and your friends, personal shopping appointments, and the two things I love the most are savings with free hemming and 20% off for all students with a valid ID! That would almost make me wanna go back to school.

Express - www.express.com

Express has been providing fashion-forward, sophisticated clothing to men and women for thirty years. It's a great place to find fashionable, tailored pieces at affordable prices. Their looks are inspired from the hottest runway trends, personally I love their men's shirts and they are also known for their fantastic fitting women's pants. For anyone who loves to look great and dress to impress whether it is work or play the fashion is definitely transitional. With over 550 stores and an online shop with must have basic wardrobe items including tanks and tees, the opportunities are endless. They have really encompassed great style with wardrobe essentials in a plethora of color options in each style. You will never be far from trendy in Express' stylish apparel. When I find a style that fits me or one of my clients here, its so affordable I often buy it in more than one color.

Forever 21 - www.forever21.com

Forever 21 is the go-to destination for ultra style-savvy and uber trendy looks at an impossible to beat price. The chain has quickly become the source for the most current fashions at the greatest value. The inventory at these stores is large and ever-changing which might make for a slightly daunting shopping experience, but put your most fashionable foot forward because you are guaranteed to find something special! Also check out their accessories department for even more cheap and cheerful pieces to update any wardrobe!

French Connection - *usa.frenchconnection.com*

A long time standard for finding fun, edgy pieces that look more high fashion than ready to wear. They have a huge variety of cuts and styles so no matter what kind of girl you feel like being, an embroidered sundress wearing girl next door or a high drama, asymmetrical shift dress flaunting vixen you can find something to suit all of your different style identities. Make sure to pick up some of their cute bags and colorful accessories to compliment your great new looks.

Gap - *www.gap.com*

Gap has always been a staple for classic khakis or a great fitting button down but in the last few years they have transformed their tried and true brand to include more updated styles and trendier looks. With their separate stores for men, woman, children, babies, and even expectant moms you can shop for the whole family and family-to-be. They have recently paired with design superstar Stella McCartney to create a lust worthy collection of clothing for kids. With their wide variety of functional yet sexy bras and panties and camisoles at Gap Body, you can literally find everything you need from start to finish at the Gap.

H&M - *www.hm.com*

It goes without saying that H&M is known as one of the most on-trend and fashion forward fast fashion retailers. The label has truly taken over the world. The chain now operates in 34 countries and manages to continually bring the runway to the realway. This is one of your best bets for a stylish pick-me-up piece. Choose from a broad selection of garments and accessories for women, men, teens, and children. And with regular limited-time collaborations with high-end designers like Matthew Williamson, Stella McCartney, Sonia Rykiel, Viktor + Rolf, Roberto Cavalli, and Japanese designer Comme des Garcons shoppers are able to own of-the-moment high style looks for a fraction of the price. They even put their most fashionable foot forward into the designer shoe arena with an exceptionally priced spotlight, guest collection of shoes from my pal Tamara at Jimmy Choo.

JCrew - *www.jcrew.com*

The iconic American brand known worldwide for its clean cut sophistication and prepster looks has stepped up it's fashion quotient even more in the last couple years. Style stars like Jewel and our favorite first lady Michelle Obama wearing their clothes has catapulted them into the fashion forefront. And it's not just about the clothes, fashionistas all about town are oooing and cooing over their vintage inspired jewelery with a modern twist which parallels the priciest of designer jewelers but at a fraction of the cost. Their accessories are fun, flirty, and fabulous as well. They have a fantastic rewards program when you open a JCrew credit card. For every $500 you spend using the card online, in-store, or by catalog, you receive a $25 rewards card. I think its fantastic that students with valid ID receive 10% off any purchase, so it is easy to be fashionable and frugal.

Levi's - *www.levis.com*

As American as apple pie, Levi's has been providing durable, classic denim since 1853. They offer everything from their classic 501s to a form-fitting high rise or low rise skinny jean. Now more than ever jeans are a staple in everyone's wardrobe, from day to night, so having the right fit is of the utmost importance. This is why it's one of my favorite places to send family and friends because with their petite, plus, and junior sections Levi's makes it easy to find a great fitting pair no matter what your size, shape, or style is. You can also find adorable dresses, skirts, shirts, and shorts with the same great styling and detail that has made Levi's a classic. Don't forget to pick up one of their iconic denim jackets, it's a must-have in any rebel's wardrobe.

Mango - *www.mango.com*

Started in Spain, this fast fashion retail store offers on-trend affordable items with a European edge. Monica Cruz, Penelope Cruz's sister, designs for the store, lending a Latin style fusion that is both fun and flirty.

Not Your Daughter's Jeans - *www.nydj.com*

The name pretty much says it all. NYDJ is an alternative to the youth oriented denim on the market today. It was developed to offer fashionable, figure flattering styles that accentuate a more mature women's assets and show off her curves. You can share lots of things with your daughter, but jeans doesn't have to be one of them.

New York & Co - *www.nyandcompany.com*

They are all about offering great style for a great price. They specialize in fashionable women's apparel and accessories without the hefty price tag. You can find everything from denim to suits to outerwear at NY&Co. It's a perfect place to shop if you are feeling like any one of the girls in Sex and the City but without having the designer budget. After all one day you feel a little Carrie and one day you feel a little Samantha and we've all felt a little Charlotte or even Miranda on different days. This is the place to go for whatever urban woman you want to be. You can look like a million bucks without having to spend a million bucks.

Old Navy - *http://oldnavy.gap.com*

A one-stop shop for the whole family, the prices at Old Navy are hard to beat. They have a huge selection of fashionable, inexpensive designs so you can look cute and trendy without spending a lot of money. They have expanded their collection to include fashion forward maternity and baby lines and they even offer a great selection of plus sized apparel exclusively online. Their designs have continued to evolve into a hip in season look at the right price point. And if you catch one of their end of season sales items can go for as low as 99 cents!

TopShop - *www.topshop.com*

Long an institution in Europe, the US has finally been invited to join this sensational fashion insider party! An incredible trend-based chain, TopShop offers a wide range of up-to-the-minute clothing for both men and women as well as an accessories and shoe department that is beyond compare. The store has also set up an e-commerce site in the US, allowing anyone across the country access to their great buys. Kate Moss was a predominant design inspiration for this company as well. Her modern, trendy line lands well at attainable prices.

Uniqlo - *www.uniqlo.com*

While this chain provides basic casual clothes and wardrobe staples with an urban edge, they are probably best known for their affordable cashmere offered in all the colors of the rainbow. You can find each great item they carry in a bagillion different colors. While there is only one location in the US—New York—the chain is growing fast and already has several expansions in the works. Their website is easy to navigate, with thousands of items categorically divided for preliminary shopping, so once you are in store sorting through their many items it's is as painless as possible. Jil Sander designed a line called Uniqlo + J as well, where she has elaborated and added signature to their staple collection.

Urban Outfitters - *www.urbanoutfitters.com*

A trendy go-to spot for the city hipster, Urban Outfitters offers slouchy chic looks for a reasonable price. With more than 130 stores in the United States, Canada, and Europe, the chain offers an eclectic mix of merchandise from women's and men's apparel to home goods and accessories. Much like its sister store, Anthropologie, Urban Outfitters is a lifestyle brand that appeals to the subversive grunge rebel in all of us.

White House Black Market - *www.whitehouseblackmarket.com*

White House started in 1985 as a small boutique in Baltimore that specialized in white and ivory clothing. In 1995 they opened White House's counterpart, Black Market, and two years later merged the two stores to create White House Black Market. They believe in the honest simplicity of black and white and the individuality that the wardrobe staples can create. It's a great place to find figure flattering designs . . . and not to worry, they do allow a little color to seep into the mix here and there.

Zara - *www.zara.com*

One of Europe's most successful Fast Fashion outposts, Zara offers a fantastic assortment of looks pulled from the runway. Now in the US as well, be sure to look for pieces to spice up any work day or weekend wardrobe. The chain's ability to translate from runway to realway is always quick, seamless, and uncanny. Their prices are slightly higher than other fast fashion retailers, but they have a knack for hitting the trends and giving daytime outfits a little extra drama, and disco diva/divos a little extra kick to their look.

Full Figure Fashion

Lane Bryant - *www.lanebryant.com*

The emphasis at Lane Bryant is on fashion and fit, not on size. You can always find fashion forward and flattering apparel for daytime divas, fashion evolved executives, and tempestuous temptresses in every curvaceous size. They even offer jewelry and accessories to accent or transition any look from day to evening. Lane Bryant also offers an exclusive intimates collection from Cacique that specializes in fit solutions and fashion styling in bras, panties, sleepwear, and more. They are known for their fantastic coupons and deals, usually available online. I've even found times when they have great giveaway gifts with purchase or special 2 for 1 offers.

Marina Rinaldi - *www.marinarinaldi.com*

Italian designer Marina Rinaldi presents sophisticated, flattering, and flirty fashion for plus sizes. With stores all across the world, it is a great place to find clothes for almost any occasion. She pays big attention to small details for the full figured fashionista, bringing any women of any size a sense of high fashion luxury. Without a doubt, her fashion is for the woman with a fabulous sense of style, but is frustrated with the limited full figured fashion options. If a store isn't accessible to your locale, Saks Fifth Avenue's Salon Z spotlights her designs along with a plethora of other chic designers.

One Stop Plus - *www.onestopplus.com*

One Stop Plus was created as the world's first online fashion mall for plus sizes. They offer over 10,000 products in over 70 sizes from the leading American and European Designers. They cater to a wide variety of clientel from the young and hip, to the trendy it girl, to the serious shopper on a budget. Whether you're running around with the kids or hobnobbing with the bigwigs at work, you will find the right looks for all your different fashion personalities here. They even carry bathing suits by one of my favorite designing women, Delta Burke. They have a very comprehensive website that includes style guides and fashion tips to enhance your shopping experience. They also have a great return policy just in case your purchases aren't quite right.

Silhouettes - *www.silhouettes.com*

Silhouettes offers an extensive collection of figure flattering designs starting at size 12W. They have a huge selection of apparel and accessories as well as a comprehensive shoe section that specializes in x-wide widths and boots that accommodate larger calves. For frequent shoppers Silhouettes offers a Buyer's Club Program. For an annual fee of $29.95 you get 10% off of every purchase you make. They also offer 20% off of your first order for joining their mailing list.

Places For Petite Picks

Ann Taylor - *www.anntaylor.com*

Ann Taylor is a great place to find figure flattering options for petite sizes. Each piece in their petite collection is perfectly proportioned to fit a smaller frame, but with a big fashion sense. You can always find the simplest pieces in a classic silhouettes or a little something special with a more fashion-forward twist. If you are looking for suits or business attire, no need to look any further, the Ann Taylor boutiques, outlets, and online stores have a wide array to choose from. Their clothes are comfortable, career minded, clean cut, and are stunningly stylish classics. They have recently teamed up with

InStyle magazine to create some of my favorite Wear to Work Chic trends, that spotlight this seasons must have pieces.

Eileen Fisher - *www.eileenfisher.com*

If you are on the petite side, not to worry you can find plenty of things to shop for from Eileen Fisher's beautiful collection of figure flattering apparel and accessories. Her signature silhouettes made from beautiful, natural fabrics have a luxurious feel and flow and yet are perfectly proportioned to fit a smaller frame. She has a very user-friendly website that contains an easy to find petite section and even offers a personal shopping service!

Nordstrom - *http://shop.nordstrom.com*

Nordstrom offers a very comprehensive selection of petite apparel. It offers a wide variety of petite collections from top designers in one convenient location. They even have the hard to find Petite Plus section that caters to fuller figured yet petite women. With such notable designer brands as Ann Klein, Ralph Lauren, and BCBG, their fashion selections are varied for women of all ages and uses from coats to dresses they've got it all for the petite purveyor fashionista.

For Moms To Be ⌒

A Pea in the Pod - *www.apeainthepod.com*

Just because you are pregnant doesn't mean you need to forgo looking fashionable and fabulous. You can pick from a huge selection of stylish maternity wear from designers such as Diane Von Furstenberg, Ella Moss, 7 For All Mankind, and Lilly Pulitzer. You can also find a stylish collection of hard to fit items like swimwear, lingerie, and work clothes, as well as support belts and shapers to keep you looking and feeling good.

H&M - *www.hm.com*

A great place to find affordable yet fashionable maternity wear, and let's face it, you're only pregnant for nine months, so why spend a lot money when you'd rather spend the money on cute outfits for the baby?

For information see listing under *Fast and Fashionable*.

Liz Lange - *www.lizlange.com*

A beautiful collection of stylish, high-end maternity clothes that you will lust over even if you aren't expecting. Liz Lange is a Hollywood favorite for moms to be. She has expanded her line to include a stylish collection of diaper bags, and in her upcoming collection she will be featuring adorable items for babies and children too. If you love Liz Lange's designs but are looking to spend a little less you're in luck! My friend has recently partnered up with my colleagues at Target to create an extra chic but less expensive line of clothing and swimwear for the Mama to be! *Available at all Target stores nationwide and online.*

Old Navy - *www.oldnavy.gap.com*

A wonderful, low cost option for all of your maternity needs, for any time of the year, for any shape or size in any part of your pregnancy. They offer hard to beat prices and cute, fashionable maternity wear. It's a great place for post pregnancy and transitional body shape shopping too.

For more information see listing under *Fast and Fashionable*.

Department Stores

Belk - *www.belk.com*

With over 300 stores spanning across 16 southern states, Belk, Inc is the nation's largest privately owned mainline department store company. They carry a large selection of clothing and accessories for men, women, and children, as well as shoes, beauty products, and home furnishings. They offer great style at an extra great value featuring a wide variety of different designer brands at affordable prices, including my girl Jessica Simpson, Kenneth Cole, Lauren by Ralph Lauren, Lucky Brand, Nine West, Calvin Klein, Jones New York, and Tahari.

Bloomingdale's - *www.bloomingdales.com*

One of the great institutions, Bloomingdales has long held a reputation for excellent selection, for men, women, and everything in between and they are know for their abundance of customer service, and constant rotation of sales. It is a fave for us stylists in New York, it's a great go to shopping point! The store is a fantastic destination for any number of products. Be sure to check out the women's apparel floor which always offers a comprehensive assortment of today's best mid to high-end labels like Catherine Malandrino, Vince, BCBG, Tracey Reese, Rebecca Taylors and more. This store is so big in Manhattan they actually have two different shoe departments, high-end and medium tier. With a Bloomingdale's credit card, if you are a Premier Plus or Ultimate Premier Insider, you can earn rewards certificates that can be used like cash at Bloomingdale's with no merchandise exceptions. For each purchase you make at Bloomie's, 3% of that purchase will go towards your Rewards Certificate. Every time you accumulate $25 worth of Rewards, you will receive a Rewards Certificate for that amount.

Dillards - *www.dillards.com*

Dillard's ranks among the nation's largest fashion apparel and home furnishings retailers. With approximately 320 locations across 29 states, the chain offers apparel for men, women, and children as well as bedding, bath, and other housewares and home goods. Designers available include BCBG, Ellen Tracy, Kenneth Cole, and Laundry by Shelli Segal. And with a Dillard's Rewards credit card, you can earn points towards your next purchase. Earn 1 point for every dollar spent on your card and gain access to cardholder-only events and sales.

JC Penney - *www.jcp.com*

One of America's leading retailers, JC Penney's offers the largest apparel and home furnishing site on the Internet as well as the nation's largest general merchandise catalog business. Keep your eye out for casual apparel, accessories, and homeware collections from some of today's leading designer names like Charlotte Ronson, Kimora Lee Simons/Baby Phat, Bisou Bisou by Michelle Bohobot, and Cindy Crawford. My home girl Cindy shares her amazing sense of style with a beautiful line of home décor items, ranging from sheets and carpets to windows and home accessories. JC Penney's also offers a significant Rewards Program. Customers are able to earn points for every dollar they spend either at the store, in the catalog, or online. Certain months are designated Double Points Month where you are able to earn twice as many points. In addition, if you earn 250 points in a month, members automatically receive a $10 credit towards their next purchase.

Kohl's - *www.kohls.com*

With the exclusive addition of Vera Wang's Simply Vera collection, Kohl's has become a destination for style-savvy shoppers across the nation. Currently, Kohl's operates stores in more than 40 states, with more than 900 locations nationwide. They partner with name brand and celebrity designers like Candie's, LC by Lauren Conrad, Levi's, Dockers, Adidas, and Daisy Fuentes to offer fashionable styles at affordable prices. Applying for a Kohl's credit card will save you 10% on your next purchase as well as extra discounts throughout the year of and extra 15 to 30% on regular and sale merchandise.

Macy's - *www.macys.com*

With over 800 locations across the nation, Macy's has long been known as one of the best bets when it comes to shopping for mid to high range brand names. The company's flagship store at Herald Square in New York City has held the title of Largest Store on Earth since 1924. So you can imagine that the labels available would be as expansive. Go to Macy's for established American designer names like Michael Kors, Tommy Hilfiger, Calvin Klein, and DKNY. But also be sure to check out their company/celebrity labels, including INC, Charter Club, Jessica Simpson, Donald Trump, and even Martha Stewart. These collections have gotten a fashion boost in recent years and offer trendy pieces at an affordable price. For frequent shoppers, the Macy's Rewards program, entitled Elite Star Rewards, allows you to earn 2% rewards on all Macy's purchases towards periodical Star Rewards Certificates. With the Macy's Elite Star card, you can earn 10% off your initial purchase as well as take advantage of 18 free special services per year, including gift wrapping, alterations, and package delivery.

Sears - *www.sears.com*

Sears offers consumers a wide range of leading brand names on any number of staple items from apparel to household goods, including, Land's End, singer LL Cool J, to Kenmore and Maytag. With its e-commerce site, comprehensive catalog distribution, and numerous outlets across the US, Sears has become one of the most trusted department store names with great customer service. Their consistent collections both for fashion, home, and even car makes Sears a place to go for any thing you need in any shape or size you want.

Specialty Department Stores

Barneys New York - *www.barneys.com*

A long time staple for fashionistas and clothing connoisseurs, Barneys is the place to go to find high-end, cutting edge, designer apparel and accessories. Their collection of ultra hip fashion from around the world makes it a favorite pick among celebrities and stylists. You can peruse through floors of Dries Van Noten, Givenchy, John Paul Gaultier, and Anne Demeulemeester. You can also lust over their enviable collection of vintage jewelry before picking up some Crème de Corps from the Kiehls counter. Simon Doonan's window displays are legendary and their signature restaurant Fred is a place to meet, greet, and be seen. Although Barneys began in New York, they can now be found in major cities nationwide. If you enroll in their "Free Stuff" card program every $1 you spend on your Barneys New York credit card earns you 1 point towards free stuff.

Bergdorf Goodman - *www.bergdorfgoodman.com*

A New York institution, Bergdorf Goodman is the place to go for luxurious items you can't find anywhere else. Each floor is dedicated to a specific category, so you can look through designer accessories, apparel, couture, evening wear, shoes, sportswear, and contemporary home furnishings in a serene, uncomplicated environment. If you need a little pick me up after all that shopping you can enjoy a delicious meal at one of their four fabulous restaurants. You can also wander across the street to the Bergdorf Goodman Men's Store where you will find an enormous collection of beautiful and fashionable menswear. Make sure to sign up for Bergdorf Goodman's rewards program to earn points towards gift cards, airline miles, and unique gifts every time you use your Bergdorf Goodman credit card. The card does not act as a credit card, but it can be used at both Bergdorf Goodman and it's sister store, Neiman Marcus.

Neiman Marcus - *www.neimanmarcus.com*

Neiman Marcus has been providing luxurious clothing, accessories, personal care products, and home furnishings for over a century. They offer high-end, apparel and accessories for women, men, and even children from famed designers such as Gucci, Marchesa, Dior, Stella McCartney, Rachel Roy, and Hervé Léger. If you want to feel pretty from head to toe you can head to their inviting makeup counters to look through the most exclusive collections of makeup and skincare lines. They also offer a competitive rewards program that lets you earn points towards gift cards, airline miles, and unique gifts every time you use your Neiman Marcus card. The card does not act as a credit card, but it can be used at both Neiman Marcus and it's sister store, Bergdorf Goodman.

Saks Fifth Avenue - *www.saksfifthavenue.com*

Renowned for its services and selection, Saks truly is one of best department stores out there. Offering American and European high-end designer names at over 50 stores across 25 states, Saks will always be a recommended destination for high-end products for men, women, and children. In addition, the department store is known for their seasonal sales with discounts of up to 70% off regular retail prices.

Saks credit card: Saks has one of the best rewards credit card programs I have seen. You can use your card in the store to earn points towards gift certificates that accumulate at the end of the year. You can then use these certificates on future purchases. Be sure to watch for Triple Points Days. Based on how much you spend, you can be entitled to different levels of membership, with even more bonuses and benefits. If you sign up for a Saks Master-Card you can earn points towards the SAKSFIRST program both inside and outside the store, just be sure to remember it is an actual credit card not just a store card.

More Bling For Less Bucks

Etsy - *www.etsy.com*
You will find an amazing collection of one-of-a-kind, handmade, and vintage items on this great little site featuring independent artists and designers. You can find almost anything here from clothing to accessories, beauty products to furniture, artwork to ceramics, and even plants and artisanal edibles. Their wide selection of jewelry is particularly impressive. They have everything from plastic baubles to meticulously crafted, fine gold, silver, and platinum jewelry. You can find a lust worthy collection of necklaces, bracelets, and ear-rings fashioned out of repurposed vintage chains and charms that have an heirloom quality but at a great price. I love that you can find pieces you can't find anywhere else here and that by shopping here you are supporting small designers.

Laila Rowe - *www.lailarowe.com*
With the constantly changing trends, it is often hard to find jewelry at a price point as realistic as the reality that you will only be wear-ing it for a season. Laila Rowe has really captured this reality with hip, trendy, and most definitely affordable accessories. With a varied selection of jewelry, shoes, scarves and bags, and in between this is a must-see site for all of your accessory essentials.

Ross-Simons - *www.ross-simons.com*
Ross-Simons has established themselves as a source for the very best in affordable jewelry and luxury gifts. Their retail stores are lo-cated predominantly on the East coast, but they have an extensive online store offering one-of-a-kind items, gold, silver, diamonds, and

other magnificent gems. Celebrity designer and friend Christie Brinkley has a fresh, sophisticated, and glamorous line offered exclusively at Ross-Simons. The pieces have classic versatility at real life prices. And with their Daily Super Deals, you can find great pieces at extremely discounted prices every day of the week!

Ultra Diamonds - *www.ultradiamonds.com*

When it comes to sparkle, this is a little luxurious splurge to save, why not take it over the top with top quality without spending a lot with Ultra Diamonds? They pride themselves on selling their product at "What Diamonds Should Cost"; you're paying for the diamond not the color of the box. Their online site and stores across the country provide high quality jewelry at prices that are accessible to the masses. With discounts up to 80%, 30 day online return, and live customer service chat, Ultra Diamonds makes your sparkle shopping as stress free as it can be! They offer a varied selection of jewelry ranging from engagement rings to personalized pieces and even exclusive designer collections. Not in the mood for diamonds? Not to worry, they don't just have diamonds; they have plethora of precious metals and gemstones as well! Ultra Diamonds has gotten real clarity, offering an immense selection of pieces at the right price for anyone in your life. Simply great bling for your buck!

For more fashionable jewelry and accessory solutions:

See *Fast Yet Fashionable* section

Anthropologie

Express

Forever 21

H & M

J Crew

New York & Co

Urban Outfitters

See *Places For Petite Picks* section

Ann Taylor

See *Big Box Stores* section

Target

Men's Stores ⌒

Men's Warehouse - *www.menswearhouse.com*

Known for their huge selection and unbeatable prices, you can browse through name brand suits, shirts, slacks, denim, accessories, shoes, sportswear, and formalwear online or at one of their 500 locations. They also carry a large selection of big and tall sizes at all of their retail locations so you are sure to find something just right for you. Because fit is important at Men's Warehouse, they offer tailoring services and style advice to ensure that you look and feel your very best.

Thomas Pink - *www.thomaspink.com*

At Thomas Pink it's all about the perfect shirt. Whether you are looking for something classic or contemporary, patterned or plain, casual or formal, you are sure to find a style that is perfect for you. Their well tailored shirts fit like they were made to your measurements, but if you're looking for a more personalized cut you can have your shirt custom-made for you through their Personally Pink service. If you don't have a Thomas Pink location in your area, not to worry, you can head over to your local Macy's where they carry a variety of their designs.

Rochester Big & Tall - *www.rochesterclothing.com*

With over 20 worldwide locations and an ecommerce site, getting fashionable clothes that fit right has never been so easy. You can choose from name brands like Burberry and Ralph Lauren as well as Cole Haan and Calvin Klein. They have all the basics like shirts, denim, swimwear, outerwear, underwear, and accessories and they even have a few hard to find items like suspenders, belts, footwear, and formalwear. Just because you don't fall into a conventional size category doesn't mean you can't look your best.

One Stop Plus (Men's Big and Tall) - *www.onestopplus.com*

Regardless of what time of day you feel like shopping their easy to navigate website makes it fast, fun, and stress free. For the man who might want some shopping assistance they also offer a 24 hour customer service line to help make shopping as painless as possible. With classic cuts, quality fabrics, and a wide array of color options to choose from, it's easy to find great fitting, timeless pieces that will keep you looking your best. Their items are affordably priced with few items reaching over $40, and with their OSP Shopper's Club risk free annual membership of $19, you can get $3 shipping and exclusive discounts!

Big Box Stores

K-Mart - www.kmart.com

K-Mart has successfully compiled a one stop shop with tons of variety for almost anything for your personal or home needs. K-Mart offers deeply discounted prices on everything from clothing to power tools. You can find the brands you love and trust without having to spend a lot of money. They feature Jaclyn Smith's exquisite designs in clothing, bathing suits, and home goods along with Kathy Ireland's Tribeca loft inspired furniture and candles. K-Mart has definitely spotlighted quality designers to withhold their standards, offering clothing in all sizes, children's (with plus size options), juniors, men, women, big and tall, husky and slim, no matter what your body type, home style, or appetite they will have it. Clothing, furniture, non-perishables, no biggie they've got it!

Target - www.target.com

Designer collaborations with the likes of such high-end labels as Zac Posen, Jean Paul Gaultier, Proenza Schouler, Thakoon, Luella Bartley, and Libertine as well as the introduction of a new trendier youth label call GO! International, have allowed Target to truly step into the spotlight as a powerhouse, fast fashion destination. Starting with their now infamous partnership with famed New York fashion designer, Isaac Mizrahi, the department store offers products at affordable prices with a definite eye for trends and aesthetic. With an easy to use sizing chart available on their website, the option to shop by specific occasion or even color, and quick shipping, there isn't much Target doesn't have to offer. In select locations, they even sell Wine Cubes, average selections in three liter bottles at affordable prices. Pair that with Archer Farm's European inspired food line and you have an instant no fuss, high class set up. With designer fashion, home goods, and affordable healthy food how could you go wrong?

Walmart - *www.walmart.com*

The behemoth of all discount department stores, Walmart is infamous for their brand names at bargain prices. Make this your destination if you need to stock up on the basics, whether in household goods, apparel, or even groceries. While Target offers the customer a slightly more edited and design-savvy assortment of goods, Walmart is the tried, tested, and true go-to for the bare necessities that won't break the bank. And with over 3400 locations worldwide, they're hard to miss!

Stores With Membership Programs

Costco - *www.costco.com*

For a $50 annual membership fee you can have access to huge savings at this highly popular megastore. With an awesome online component and over 550 locations you can find everything under the sun and more! You can stock up on food, furniture, sheets, towels, and flooring, among countless other high quality, low cost items. The selection of electronics with fantastic warranties really set them apart from many of the other big box stores. And if you want to pick up a diamond with that stereo set you're in luck. You can find a top-notch collection of high quality jewelry at great prices! You can literally find almost anything you could possibly want here, from fresh seafood to garden sheds.

Sam's Club - *www.samsclub.com*

By keeping their overhead low, Sam's Club, a Walmart corporation, can offer amazing savings on basic, everyday household items. With an option for in store pick up or home delivery, your shopping experience can be fast and hassle-free. It is a bulk-buying bonanza at

Sam's Club, where you can find items to furnish your house or even your own bed and breakfast or motel. All products are accessible online and in stores across the country. Members can enjoy a personal shopper option, where you can order online and pick up your purchase the next day to avoid long lines and potential chaos at the high volume warehouse. Whether it's in store or online, the deals are sparkling just like their diamond collection.

Sephora - *www.sephora.com*

Featuring over 200 brand names in cosmetics and beauty, this highly popular open-sell store boasts over 510 stores in 14 countries worldwide and 250 in North America. The Sephora Beauty Insider Program is free to join and earns you points per purchase. You also receive free samples and product gifts with every purchase and a special present on your birthday.

Organic/Green Shopping

Eco-Chick - *http://eco-chick.com*

Eco-Chick is a fabulous source for how to adopt a more sustainable lifestyle. The site offers easy alternatives to conventional products and shows that you don't have to spend a lot of money and sacrifice style to be green. In addition to the site you can also get great tips in Starre Vartan's book *The Eco-Chick Guide to Life: How to be Fabulously Green*.

Green Depot - *www.greendepot.com/greendepot*

See *Stores for Closet Organization* section

Nimli - *www.nimli.com*

Nimli is devoted to providing natural, organic, and sustainable lifestyle products while maintaining style. The site sells everything from clothing to home décor to beauty products to accessories by independent designers such as Toggery, Cri de Coeur, and Angel-Rox. All products are recycled, sweatshop free, and cruelty free and if that's not enough they offer weekly sales on their site and free shipping on all orders over $100.

Skin Deep Cosmetics Safety Database - *www.cosmeticsdatabase.com*

Cosmetics Database is an online safety guide for cosmetics and personal care products. It is an incredibly comprehensive site that allows you to make informed decisions about what you put on your body. Each product is assigned a number from 0 (nontoxic) to 10 (very toxic) and has a brief summary so you know exactly what is in each product and why or why not it may be harmful. Until cosmetics companies are forced to be more honest about what they are putting in their products, the Cosmetics Database arms you with the knowledge you need to make healthy and informed decisions about what you buy.

The Green Loop - *www.thegreenloop.com*

A fantastic site offering sustainable fashion made by conscientious companies who are committed to going green. The designs by new and emerging names such as Edun, Stewart+Brown, and Perfectly Imperfect are completely stylish and fashion forward.

You can look good and feel good when you shop at The Green Loop.

White Apricot - *www.whiteapricot.com*

A fantastic online newsletter for all the latest trends, news, and information on eco fashion, bodycare, and other green products and services. They highlight the latest shoes, jewelry, and clothing from hot eco-designers like Loyale, Melissa, and Kelly B. They also have a great section for exclusive offers where you can find discounts for up to 70% from all of the eco companies you know and love.

Canadian Stores

Holt Renfrew - *www.holtrenfrew.com*

A Canadian staple in the luxury market for over 170 years Holt Renfrew is the place to go to find the latest designer apparel and accessories for men and women. You can shop for the latest looks from mega designers like Céline, Dolce and Gabbana, Marc by Marc Jacobs, and Michael Kors. Their stores offer full service shopping experience. With concierge services, personal shoppers, a full service salon and spa, and a café, you won't need to go anywhere else.

The Shoe Company - *www.theshoecompany.com*

The Shoe Company, a subsidiary of Town Shoes, one of Canada's leading shoe retailers prides itself on being the number one family shoe store in Canada. Offering multiple brand selections ranging from Timberland and Nike to Madden Girl it has styles the whole family can enjoy. Their sizing is extremely large, offering men's shoes up to size 16. Each store carries 20,000 pairs of brand name shoes, and a huge collection of handbags, sunglasses, hats, clothing, socks, umbrellas, shoe care products, and other great accessories. Their prices are great and they often have special promotions both in store and online regularly.

Town Shoes - *www.townshoes.com*

Town Shoes and The Shoe Company are linked together through both of their websites making shopping for any price, size, or style easier than ever. Town Shoes is where all the fashionistas head to get name brand shoes for reasonable prices. This 50 year old company does a great job staying fashion forward and fresh with their choice of brand buying with brands such as Diesel, BCBG Girls, Lacoste, Ugg, Franco Sarto, and Hush Puppies. You can find a comprehensive collection of name brand men's and women's shoes as well as a stylish array of accessories. The prices are slightly higher than their offshoot store, The Shoe Company, but they offer great promotions and in store incentives.

Winners - *www.winners.ca*

Part of TJX Companies Inc, Winners is the Canadian counterpart to TJ Maxx, Marshalls, and Homegoods. They offer designer finds at huge discounts. They strive to negotiate the greatest deals so that the incredible savings can be passed down to their customers.

With their helpful style guides and trend reports you will have no trouble putting together fun, fashionable outfits for $40 to $70(and that includes shoes and accessories!). After you go to Winners you will never want to pay full price again.

Stores For Closet Organization ⌒

Bed Bath & Beyond - *www.bedbathandbeyond.com*

Bed Bath & Beyond has a great, mid-priced selection of modular closet systems. You can mix and match to create exactly what you need so that your closet is set up exactly how you want it to be. A big part of having an organized closet is making sure all of your off season clothing is nicely stored and put away. Bed Bath & Beyond's extensive garment storage options will keep your off season items sorted, protected and well organized until you are ready to wear them again. Bed Bath & Beyond has everything you could possibly need to accommodate all of your storage needs.

Green Depot - *www.greendepot.com/greendepot*

An extremely comprehensive site and store for eco-friendly and sustainable building supplies, services, and home furnishings. Their primary goal is to facilitate green living and building in communities so that it is easy, affordable, and gratifying. Whether you are looking to repaint your living room, renovate your bathroom, or buy some bedding for your baby's new crib Green Depot has it all.

Ikea - *www.ikea.com*

If you are looking for an inexpensive closet system, Ikea is a great place to go. The selection isn't huge, but you can get a basic, customizable system for a fraction of the cost. You can also find a wide selection of free standing closet systems and shoe organizers there, so if you have an inadequate closet or no closet at all you can create a well organized, sleek looking set up from their wide selection of streamlined furniture.

Home Depot - *www.homedepot.com*

For the creative, more competent individual, Home Depot offers all the right components to supply you with everything you need to create the closet of your dreams. With systems from brands like ClosetMaid, John Louis Home, John Sterling, and Martha Stewart Living you can find the right style at the right price no matter what your budget. Whether you're retrofitting your dorm room or redoing your master bedroom you can definitely find what you are looking for here. You can also pick up all the tools and supplies you need to complete your job so if you come in prepared, and don't get side-tracked by the aisles and aisles of merchandise, you can get everything you need in one trip.

Lowe's - *www.lowes.com*

This home improvement mega store has versatile, inexpensive options to help you get your closet into peak organizational condition. They have customizable wire closet organizers, wood closet organizers, cubes, drawers, shoe storage, racks, and wardrobes. It offers a slightly more comfortable shopping experience for the intimidated, first time do-it-yourselfer and if you need a little extra help or inspiration you can head over to the Lowe's website where you can find easy to follow assembly instructions videos and design ideas. You might start with your closet, but after a few runs around the store you may get inspired to redo your whole house!

The Container Store - *www.containerstore.com/welcome.htm*

Junk drawers and unruly piles will be a thing of the past once you set foot in this organizational super store. You can purchase an entire, built in closet system from elfa here or you can purchase the components individually if your organizational needs are on the smaller side. The staff is very knowledgeable and helpful and will walk you through the entire process to make sure you get exactly what you want. You can also choose from an extensive collection of storage bins and clothes hangers as well as shoe organizers, garment storage bags, and accessories organizers. With a store like this there is no excuse for a messy closet anymore!

Nationwide Charities

Big Brothers and Big Sisters - *www.bbbs.org*

Big Brothers and Big Sisters is the oldest, largest, and most effective youth-mentoring organization in the United States. As a leader in the one-to-one youth service for more than a century, the organization's goal is to have a direct and lasting effect on the lives of under-privileged youths and mentors children from ages 6 to 18 at locations across the country. Each child enrolled in the program is assigned their own personal mentor who will help them to reach their potential.

Cinderella Project - *www.cinderellaproject.net*

The Cinderella Project accepts donations of new and used formal dresses and gowns as well as accessories to allow young disadvantaged women to attend their high school proms and other formal dances without worrying about the financial burden associated with attending such events.

Dress for Success - *www.dressforsuccess.org*

The mission of Dress for Success is to promote the economic and emotional independence of disadvantaged women by providing them with professional attire and accessories for potential job interviews and meet-and-greets. On top of providing these women with appropriate attire, the organization also offers job and interview training as well as career counselors and support classes. The organization accepts donations of new and used business attire, including suits, shirts, shoes, and accessories.

Goodwill - *www.goodwill.org*

Goodwill is North America's leading nonprofit organization dedicated to providing education, career services, and training for the disadvantaged, including those on welfare, the homeless, as well as those with physical, mental, and emotional stabilities. The organization believes that through work and gainful employment, self-confidence, independence, and trust can be built. Goodwill accepts donations of clothing and household goods that are then sold in over 2000 Goodwill retail stores as well as on their Internet auction site (*www.shopgoodwill.com*). The revenue generated from their stores helps fund job training and other services.

Housing Works - *www.housingworks.org*

Housing Works is the largest community based AIDS service organization in the United States. Since 1990 they have provided housing, medical and mental health care, meals, job training, drug treatment, HIV prevention education, and social support to more than 20,000 homeless and low-income New Yorkers living with HIV and AIDS. To help pay for the services they provide Housing Works runs a number of high-end thrift stores throughout New York. You can donate clothing, accessories, and books at each of their retail locations. If you want to donate furniture they have a free pick-up program. You can also go to their website to find other ways you can help out.

Military Order of the Purple Heart - *www.purpleheartpickup.org*

The MOPH is a Congressionally chartered national veteran's service organization that funds welfare, rehabilitation, and educational programs for veterans in need. Funds for these programs are raised through the sale of donated household goods contributed through the charity's user-friendly Pick-Up Service.

Network For Good - *www.networkforgood.org*

Network for Good is the Internet's leading charitable resource, bringing together donors, volunteers, and charities to one online site. Internet users can donate to more than one million listed charities as well as search through thousands of volunteer opportunities. This site makes donating your time, money, or used items incredibly easy. If you are unsure of what charity you would like to support, this is the site to come to. Their search engine will allow you to look through directories by category and location.

Nike Reuse-A-Shoe Program - *www.nikereuseashoe.com*

Every year millions of shoes are thrown out and dumped into landfills. Through Nike's Reuse-A-Shoe program old athletic shoes are collected from a number of different sources and recycled into playing surfaces such as basketball courts, tennis courts, running tracks, soccer fields, fitness flooring, and playground safety surfacing. Since 1993 Nike has recycled more than 20 million pairs of athletic shoes and contributed to more than 250 sport surfaces. Nike also recycles most of the scrap material leftover from manufacturing their own shoes. The shoes and shoe materials are ground up into what they like to call Nike Grind. All you have to do is send in any old athletic shoes you have lying around—they don't have to be Nike—and you can help contribute to this wonderful cause.

Salvation Army - www.salvationarmyusa.org

The Salvation Army's adult rehabilitation centers provide spiritual, social, and emotional assistance for men and women who have lost the ability to cope with their current living situation, emotional problems, and are unable to provide for themselves. Each center offers residential housing, work opportunities, group and individual therapy, and clean and wholesome surroundings. The physical and spiritual care that program participants receive prepares them to re-enter society and return to gainful employment. The Work Therapy portion of the program includes the collection, repair, and sale of donated items through the Salvation Army Stores.

Soles 4 Souls - www.soles4souls.org

Soles4Souls takes donated used shoes and distributes them throughout the world to people in need. Shoe companies, retailers, and individuals can donate footwear, which will then be used in various relief efforts. The charity was onsite during the Asian tsunami, Hurricanes Katrina and Rita, and other natural disasters, handing out more than 1 million pairs of donated shoes.

The Furniture Bank Association - www.thenfba.org

The National Furniture Bank Association routes your donated furniture and kitchenware to the Partnership for the Homeless and other nonprofits that are dedicated to helping people set up and maintain their own households. Donors pay for removal of the furniture they have chosen to donate.

Vietnam Veterans of America - www.vva.org

The VVA is a national veterans service organization which serves the needs of veterans of the Vietnam War era throughout the nation.

The organization is primarily funded by fund-raising activities and membership. Another key source of funding is through the resale of donated items, including apparel and household goods. While the VVA does not own retail outlets of its own, it sells the donations through other qualified retailers.

Acknowledgments

We are better because we listen and love each other.

To those gone too soon—Marlene and Richard Bloch, Cora Bloch, Rita Baron, Ruby Schwartz, Annette Baker, Tibby, Sam, Sandra and Cindy Viner, Stanley Schwartz, Corrine Kraft, Ricky Massey, and Robin Bronfman Fischa.

To Gloria Limanni Armstrong and Pieter Estersohn—I was better because you loved me in this crazy life and these crazy times.

To the family—Caryl and Seymour Specter, Jeryl, Matt, Josh and Daniel Baker, Debbie and Steven, Abby, Matt, Ronit, Aviela and Amatai Schwartz, Eddie Viner and family.

To Alexandra Clarke whose tireless commitment, dedication, and ability to keep calm while putting out fires will always be appreciated.

To the team—those who did their job so I could do mine: Brooke Bryant, Chantel Cloutier, Strand Conover, Miles Gidaly, Jeff Googel, Glenn Gulino, Patti Kim, Madeline Leonard, Heidi Krupp Lisiten, Darren Lisiten, Suzanne Lyon, Nena Madonia, Jan Miller, Adrienne Novak, Amy Sabel, and Mark Turner.

To my favorite elves—Ryanne Kim, Carmen Mantione, Victoria Collins, Chiara Morrison, and Meredith Lovegrove.

To the Old School Homies—Perrie Halpern, Cheryl Krome, Iris Tomashaw, Mary Beth Armstrong, Elyse Richman, Linda Kotch, John Foliano, Patrick McMullan, Andra Milsome, Cindy Bier Sofer, Ethan Silverman, Jennifer George, Tania Martin, Renee Cox, Michelle Fielding, Lisa Bevis, Nicole Burdette, Gus and Maria Heningburg, and Stefano and Thea Di Sabatino.

ACKNOWLEDGMENTS

To the Home Girls who shared their hearts, humor, and homes with me—Pamela Chess, Yvette Gilpin, Cheryl Giefer, Brigid Walsh, Lauren Holly, Catherine Dent, Jeanne Becker, Lisa France, Belinda Marment, Apollonia Kotero, Claudia Cantu, Claudia Klein, Jacque Carder, Marsha Thomason-Sykes, Keisha Nash Whitaker, Milica Kennedy Kastner, Dawn Evans, Yolanda Ross, Robin Bronk, Lisa Driver, Joan Kors, Anne Vincent, Robin Kay, Rolanda Watts, Nina Rawls, Melanie Bromley, Kristen Kelly, Wendy Natale, Chrissy Iley, and Rozita Pnini.

To the Home Girls' Husbands, Kids, Sistas, and Brothas—David, Sawyer, and Charles Park Armstrong; Frank, Linda, and Connie Limanni; Matt, Madeline, and Catherine Halpern; Michael Krome; Kia, Vienna, Olivia, and Mickey Fischa; Andrea, Martin, Rebecca, Garrett, and Alexander Pouliot; Tony; Octavia, and Max; Fran Azur; George and Henry Greco; Ed, Forrest, Autumn, True, and Sonnet Whitaker; and Betty, Buddy, and Elio Estersohn.

To the Runnin' Buddies—Quohnos Mitchell, Jeff Grubb, Quinton Ford, Koby Benvenisti and Carl Reece, Dialo Reece, Craig Howard, Josh Smiling and Lyon Henry, Dale Farquharson, Everette Brown, Javier Leblanch, EZ, Carl Lewis, Trey Lorenz, Frank Gatson, Timmy Bayly, Dr. Ray Swainson, Drew Ianni, Savoy Walker, Robert Ell, Jamar, Qwynn Dolmo, Re'Shaun Frear, Dwayne Palmer, Jay Greg, Alonzo Johnson, Steve Valbrun, Sean Johnson, Tony Orea, Felix Count, and Nathan Hale Williams.

The Birthday Club—Frank Lombardi, Bennett Goldworth, Debbie Sansevero, Melinda Wiswell, and Fran Drescher.

My Fashionable Friends and to the mentors and those whose creative genius and friendship have inspired me—Ms. DeQuilfeldt, Professor Brad Zamkoff, Dr. Peter Ruane, Sacha Gambachini, Franca Sozzani, Monica Dolfini, Patti Wilson, Barbara Dente, Pat Field, Steve Alperin, Diana B, Diane Benson, Oscar Blandi, Michelle Bohbot, Kim Bondy, David Bozman, Marvet Britto, Shelly Bromfield, Brooklyn Brownstone, Alina Cho, BJ Coleman, Janet and Jimmy at Fragments, John Demsey, Simon Doonan and Julie Gilhart at Barneys, David Duralde and Don Howard at Kenmark, Louise Elard, Joanne Gair, Tracy Gray at Nike, Kathy Griffin, Desia Halprin-Brill, Barbara Horvath, Miss J., Daryn Kagen, Michael

Kerner, Judy Licht, Edie Locke, Henry Mauldin, Matthew Mellon, Luis Moro, Theo Perry, Serena Radaelli, Maureen Reidy, Monica Schenker, Michel Schneider at Clothes Off Our Back, Johanne Siff, Patty Sicular and Crystal Hunt, Mary Alice Stevenson, Edward Tricomi, Robert Verdi, Rachel Wells, Constance White, Robin Wunsh Barron, Fern Mallis, and Perez Hilton.

The Photographers—Carlo Dalla Chiesa, Andrew Eccles, Davis Factor, Daniella Federicci, Ash Gupta, George Holz, David LaChapelle, George Lange, Andrew McPherson, Tony Meneguzzo, Amery Moultry, Jon Ragel, Mathew Rolston, Mark Seliger, Andrew Southam, Randee St. Nicholas, Art Streiber, Michael Tighe, Diego Uchitel, Javier Vallhonrat, Cliff Watts, Timothy White, James White, Firooz Zahedi, and Herb Ritts.

To the Designers—my friends Catherine Malandrino and Bernard Aidan, Reem Acra, Giorgio Armani, Max and Luba Azria, Badgley Mischka, Bradley Bayou, Luisa Beccaria, Steven Burrows, Ennio Capasa at Costume National, Kenneth Cole, J'Aton Couture, Diddy, Collette Dinnigan, Tom Ford, Dolce & Gabbana, Randolph Duke, Alberta Ferretti, Diane von Furstenberg, John Galliano, Romeo Gigli, John Paul Gaultier, Tommy Hilfiger, Hush Puppies, Marc Jacobs, Betsy Johnson, Donna Karan, Martin Katz, my friends at Khiels, Eloise and Paul Mitchell, Tina Knowles and Ty Hunter, Michael Kors, Adrienne Landau, Neil Lane, Ralph Lauren, Hervé Léger, Nanette Lepore, Monique Lhuillier, Christian Louboutin, Nicole Miller, Marghcrita Missoni at Missoni, NIKE, Rifat Ozbek, Zac and Susan Posen, Bernardo Rojo for Joseph Abboud, Sergio Rossi, Rachel Roy, Ralph Rucci, Stephen Russell, Elie Saab, Lorraine Schwartz, Christian Siriano, Georges Chakra, Kimora Lee Simmons and Russell Simmons, Steven Sprouse, Elie Tahari, Vivienne Tam, Richard Tyler, Valentino, Diego della Valle, Donatella and Gianni Versace, John Varvatos, Stuart Weitzman, Say What, Heidi Wiesel, Jason Wu, Tamara Yeardye of Jimmy Choo, and the glamorous Georgina Chapman and Keren Craig at Marchesa.

Image Makers—Genevieve Ascenscio at Factory PR, Susan Ashbrook and Carla Blizzard, Michelle Bega, M Booth, Karen Bromley, Tom Cestaro at Celebrities Plus Inc, Kelly Cutrone of People's Revolution, Liz Dalling at Special Artists Agency, Carlos de Souza, Roni

Deutch, Donna Faircloth, Crissi Giamos, Marion Greenberg, Tom Handley, Marilyn Heston, Amal Kamoo, James LaForce and Lesley Stevens at LaForce + Stevens, The Lawlor Sisters, Marleah Leslie, Mary Loving, Molly Madden at 3 Arts Entertainment, Wanda Mcdaniel and Barry Frediani, Sally Morrison and the DIC, MS&L, Tom Parziale, Anamaria Pavoni and Richard Presser at Hugo Boss, Jodi Rappaport, Cindy Riccio, Carrie Ross, Pam Seidman, Trudy Larson, Kenton Selvey and Kelle Night for Joseph Abboud, Weber Shandwick PR, Susan Shin, Nick Dietz, Peggy Siegal, Michelle Stein and Lisa Lawrence at Aeffe, Kelly Stone of Scene Again, Karyn Tencer, and Danielle Thur.

My Magazine Peeps—Martha Nelson, Hilary Alexander, Jason Binn at Niche Media; Anne Bratskeir at *Newsday*; Richard Buckley, Susannah Cahn, Mark Ellwood, and Style List at Aol.com; Deidre Behar and FoxNews.com; Paul Cavaco, Glynis Costin, Ariel Foxman, Charla Lawhon, Hal Rubenstein, and Cindy Weber Cleary at *InStyle* magazine; Bonnie Fuller, Marianne Garvey, Robin Givhan, and Richard Johnson at Page Six; Mickey Boardman and Kim Hastreiter at *Paper Mag*; Susan Kaufman at *People* magazine; Gayle King at O magazine; Michael Kochman, Marylou Luther, Suzy Menkes, and Sasha Charnin Morrison at *Us Weekly*; Michael Roberts, Elizabeth Saltzman, and Punch Hutton at *Vanity Fair*; Amy Spindler and the *New York Times*; RadarOnline.com; Anna Stuart, Courtney Kierce, The Thread, and Yahoo.com; Hamish Bowles, Grace Coddington, Candy Pratts Price, Andre Leon Talley, and Anna Wintour at *Vogue*.

My Television Crews—Brad Bessey and Linda Bell at *Entertainment Tonight*; Katie Davis at *Oprah*; Jeff Olde and VH1; Janell Snowden, Katie Caperton, Jason Evans, Stephanie Minter, Jeanne Moos, Mara Wilcox, and Jennifer Wolfe at CNN; Barbara Walters and the ladies of *The View*; Regis, Kelly, and Gelman of *Live with Regis and Kelly*; Kevin Harry and *Inside Edition*; E! Entertainment Television; Style Network; Extra; MTV; Nancy Lesser and HBO; 51 Minds, Randy Barbato, and Fenton Bailey at WOW; Kalina Rahal and KTLA 5 Morning News; Jessica Golden and Katie Slaman at ABC News; Brian Neal and Tijuana.

To those stars who have shared their light so we could both sparkle brighter—Jessica Alba, Maria Conchita Alonso, Jennifer Aniston, Tyra Banks, Christie Brinkley, Pierce Brosnan and Keely Shaye, Joy Bryant, Sandy Bullock, Mariah Carey, Jim Carrey, Kim Cattrall, Courtney Cox, Cindy Crawford, Tim Daly, Cameron Diaz, Janet Dickinson, Fran Drescher, Faye Dunaway, Jenna Elfman, Giancarlo Esposito, Vivica A. Fox, Selma Hayek, Jill Hennessy and Paolo, Paris Hilton, Cheryl Hines, Rachel Hunter, Liz Hurley, Iman, Sam Jackson and LaTanya Richardson Jackson, Kristin Johnston, Regina King, Beyoncé Knowles, Jennifer Lopez, Julianna Margulies, Debi Mazar, Jenny McCarthy, Demi Moore, Garcelle Geauvais Nilon, Sarah Jessica Parker, Holly Robinson Peete, Joan Rivers, Diana Ross, Meg Ryan, Annabella Sciorra, Charlie Sheen, Jessica Simpson, Jimmy Smits, Sharon Stone, Jennifer Tilly, Michelle Trachtenberg, Kelly Preston and John Travolta, Donald Trump, Angela Bassett and Courtney B. Vance, Mark Wahlberg, Denzel Washington, Kerry Washington, Veronica Webb, Vanessa Williams, Oprah Winfrey, Jane Kazmerick and Clothes Off Our Back, Kelly and Sharon Stone's Planet Hope, Atlanta Center for the Visually Impaired, and the Creative Coalition.

And to those who allowed me to share in a part of their story and a part of history—Academy Award Winner Halle Berry and the King of Pop, Michael Jackson.

About the Author

The premier fashion stylist to the stars, Phillip Bloch works with Hollywood's A-list, including such celebrity clients as John Travolta, Sandra Bullock, Faye Dunaway, Selma Hayek, and Jada Pinkett Smith. A regular commentator on TV and contributor to publications like *Vanity Fair, Vogue, InStyle, Premiere, Entertainment Weekly, Elle, Detour,* and ABC.com (as a pop culture guru), Phillip's unique combination of expertise and humor has made him one of the most sought-after and outspoken stylists in Hollywood. And his momentum just keeps getting stronger! He's cohosted VH1's *Glam God,* partnered with Hush Puppies on their new "Guest Designer Series" collection of shoes, and has an upcoming licensing deal with DSW and Tanger Outlet.